1975

Averroes on Plato's *Republic*

Averroes on Plato's *Republic*

TRANSLATED, WITH AN INTRODUCTION
AND NOTES, BY *Ralph Lerner*

Cornell University Press

ITHACA AND LONDON

First published 1974 by Cornell University Press.
Published in the United Kingdom by Cornell University Press Ltd., 2-4 Brook Street, London W1Y 1AA.

International Standard Book Number 0-8014-0821-0
Library of Congress Catalog Card Number 73-18521

Printed in the United States of America.

Preface

You have here something close to what Abū'l-Walīd
Muḥammad Ibn Aḥmad Ibn Rushd (known to the Latins as
Averroes) wrote toward the end of the twelfth century in
Córdoba. Little more can be asserted with confidence and
candor because it may be three centuries since anyone last saw
a copy of the Arabic text. What has come down to us is a Hebrew
translation of the Arabic, composed by Samuel ben Judah in
the early fourteenth century in Provence and preserved in eight
manuscripts in varying states of completeness. Based on that
Hebrew translation, there have been one Hebrew summary (by
Joseph Caspi in 1331) and four translations—two in Latin (by
Elia del Medigo[1] in 1491 and by Jacob Mantinus[2] in 1539) and
two in English, of which this is the latest. Very much, then,
turns on the capability and accuracy of the two translators who
stand between you and the author. Samuel has already made
his apologies (see Appendix I); it only remains for me to speak
on my own behalf.

This new English translation is presented in the belief that it
marks an improvement in accuracy and intelligibility over the
pioneering critical edition and translation of E. I. J. Rosenthal.[3]

[1] "Expositio Comentatoris Averois in librum Politicorum Platonis," MS
Siena, Biblioteca Comunale degli Intronati, G VII 32, fols. 158r–188r. (I have
used enlargements from microfilm.)

[2] "Averrois Cordubensis Paraphrasis in libros de Republica Platonis," in
Aristotelis Opera cum Averrois Commentariis (Venetiia apud Junctas, 1562; reprint
ed., Frankfurt am Main: Minerva G.m.b.H., 1962), III, 334v–372v.

[3] *Averroes' Commentary on Plato's "Republic,"* University of Cambridge Oriental
Publications, no. 1 (Cambridge: Cambridge University Press, 1956; reprinted
with corrections, 1966, 1969); hereafter cited as Rosenthal.

Some of the differences in approach may be mentioned here:
(1) Rosenthal establishes his Hebrew text by using as his point
of departure an early sixteenth-century manuscript, MS B.[4] The
present translation is based in large measure on MS A[5] (dated
1457), the oldest of the extant manuscripts and one containing
a number of unique and superior readings. The strengths of this
manuscript[6] and its age entitle it to serve as the foundation of a
critical text and of its translation. But as MS A is not without its
defects, I have borrowed readings from other Hebrew manuscripts (as given in Rosenthal's *apparatus criticus* to his Hebrew
text) wherever the interests of clarity of thought and good
grammar are served. (2) Any translator, confronted with a text
as obscure, difficult, and strange as this one, is sorely tempted to
try to reconstruct a hypothetical Arabic original text and correct
the Hebrew on the basis of a presumed misreading of the Arabic
by the Hebrew translator. I have borne in mind the dangers in
such a procedure, adopting it rarely and then only with re-
luctance and caution. Samuel was acutely aware of his shortcomings as a translator of philosophic Arabic; but if his word is
to be taken in this matter, he was tireless in his efforts to provide
the reader with a translation that was faithful to Averroes and
intelligible to one who knew Hebrew but no Arabic. Moreover,
he saw what none of us has seen—Averroes' Arabic text. (3)
Rosenthal understands Averroes' intention in this work as the
"identification of the Ideal State with the Islamic, i.e. *Sharī'a*
State, and the conviction of the superiority of the religious law"
(p. 299). This understanding informs his translation and his
elaborate notes.[7] The Introduction to the present translation

[4] MS Munich, Bayrische Staatsbibliothek, Hebr. 308, fols. 1v–43v.

[5] MS Florence, Biblioteca Medicea Laurenziana, Conventi Soppressi 12,
fols. 94r–129v. (I have used enlargements from microfilm.)

[6] See the review of Rosenthal by J. L. Teicher, *Journal of Semitic Studies*, 5
(1960): 176–195, especially pp. 193 f.

[7] See the review of Rosenthal by Shlomo Pines, *'Iyyun—Hebrew Philosophical
Quarterly*, 8 (1957): 65–84.

addresses itself, among other things, to this assertion and offers an alternative interpretation.

It is a special pleasure to acknowledge publicly the help I have received from others. Every translator builds on the work of his predecessors. It is only common courtesy to acknowledge that their efforts (especially those of Rosenthal) have helped me through a tangled and by no means unambiguous text—sometimes by providing examples to follow, at other times by leading me to further reflection on Samuel's text and Averroes' intention.

I am indebted to Muhsin Mahdi for his incisive criticisms of the translation and for giving his counsel unstintingly, promptly, and with delicacy. I am also grateful to Shlomo Pines for helpful suggestions concerning some of the more obscure and intractable passages in this text.

In ways varied and many (as Averroes might say), I have drawn upon the insights and energies of my guide to the world of the *falāsifa*, Leo Strauss. This volume is dedicated to his memory.

R. L.

Chicago, Illinois

Contents

Introduction

Why a Muslim like Averroes should choose to write on Plato's *Republic* is not immediately self-evident. Of what use is this pagan closet philosophy to men who already hold what they believe to be the inestimable gift of a divinely revealed Law, a *sharī'a*? Can that Law, which presents itself as complete and sufficient and which addresses all men, the Red and the Black, be in need of supplement or correction? Further, what has the "lawyer, imām, judge, and unique scholar" (as Averroes chooses to describe himself elsewhere) to do with those matters that Plato makes the theme of the *Republic*? We know that this list of titles exhausts neither Averroes' interests nor his qualifications. Aquinas and Dante have in mind no one else when they speak of *the* Commentator on Aristotle's works. Marrākushī, in his *History of the Maghrib*, repeats a first-person account in which Averroes explains to a pupil how he was led to summarize Aristotle's works in response to the wish of the ruler Abū Ya'qūb and the urgings of the latter's chief physician and vizier, Ibn Ṭufayl. This epitome or paraphrase of the *Republic* is to be seen, then, as a part of that larger project, for as Averroes himself says at the beginning of this work, he has taken up Plato's book because Aristotle's *Politics* "has not yet fallen into our hands" (22.5). But all this, while it accounts for some things, leaves unanswered the earlier and more basic question: What is the standing of pagan philosophy in the Muslim community? We may say, with little exaggeration, that almost the first and last words of this work point to the utility, relevance, even necessity, of political science (21.7; 105.5-6). Again and again, Averroes quietly points out that this practical science, far from being superseded by the *shari'a*, is no less needed in "these cities." Just how badly needed is, in a way, one of the larger lessons of the work. Their very lack of awareness of their sickness is itself a measure of how sick these cities truly are.

Even if we accept the notion that Plato has something to teach the adherents of religious Law about the ways of preserving or restoring political health, it can hardly be said that the Plato who appears in these pages is altogether familiar. Only a detailed, point-by-point comparison of this work with the text of the *Republic* can disclose the many differences between the two. Least to be wondered at is the Islamization of the *Republic*; Greek divinities and examples are replaced by examples better known to Averroes' readers. More remarkable are the substantive discrepancies—elaborations where Plato is brief, omissions, changes in details, interpolations drawn from Aristotle or Farabi or others. How much weight ought to be given to these variations from our text of the *Republic* must remain a matter of controversy, complicated by the fact that not a single Arabic translation of a complete Platonic work is known to have come down to us. In the absence of the text that Averroes had before him when he sat down to compose this work, we can only hazard some guesses about the significance of the discrepancies. We cannot even be sure that they are departures from Plato. Judging from the Arabic translations of Greek texts that are extant, the translators did their work with intelligence and skill. Careful readers of this or of the Hebrew translation will have no difficulty in recognizing many passages that disclose great fidelity even to the nuances of Plato's text. In brief, we cannot know for a certainty whether whatever of Averroes' account strikes us as baffling or simply wrong in the light of our present-day understanding of Plato's text does so because of inadvertence or design. Averroes' thoughts may not be our thoughts.

In this age in which we are urged on all sides to flaunt whatever we believe we have, this restrained work of Averroes is triply strange. The *falāsifa* (as the medieval philosophers are called in Arabic) do not as a rule strut forth proclaiming their ingenuity, originality, and superiority over their predecessors. Quite the contrary: a good deal of their ingenuity and originality is devoted to concealing their singularities. The present text by Averroes is a fine case in point, for in truth it is no simple matter to tell in every instance whether Averroes is speaking in his own name. The gentle glidings from "he says" to "we say" and back again (with variations en route) lull the senses of the good-natured reader who nods along as Averroes repeats whatever Plato "says" or "asserts" or "holds" or "explains." Every once in a while, however, that good-natured reader is jolted by various devices into wondering where Averroes himself stands on these matters. Sometimes Averroes tells him directly; sometimes he tells him indirectly. Sometimes Averroes merely plants the question. In all cases, however, Averroes moves with boldness and determination in setting before the attentive reader the problems that matter, the problems posed by the confrontation of classical political philosophy and the *sharī'a*. The more that attentive reader sees, the better trained he becomes in understanding those problems. Much of his training consists in discerning "what we ourselves had in mind to explain" (103.15). With a view to achieving that great good, a useful first step would be to consider some examples of the different modes in which Averroes chooses to speak in his own name.

Averroes most evidently speaks in his own name when he speaks emphatically. On rare occasions he uses the first person singular, as when he reports, "I have seen many among the poets and those who grow up in these cities" who prefer tyrannical rule (101.16); or when he asserts that, despite the fact that an inquiry of a certain character would more fittingly be made in the first (i.e., scientific) part of political science, "I deem it appropriate that I mention some of it here" (65.8-9). Even rarer is Averroes' use of oaths, as when he swears—"upon my life!"—that the argument Plato has produced showing the pleasure of the intellect is the greatest pleasure is a demonstrative argument (104.25); or when he swears that another argument of Plato's is true although not demonstrative (104.29-30). The device Averroes most frequently uses for emphasis is his supplying the personal pronoun "we" to verbs whose suffixed pronominal particles already make unmistakably clear who the subject of the sentence is. The redundant pronoun may thus be understood as performing the function of italics: "We ourselves follow after him" (30.23) is tantamount to Averroes' insisting that the reader note his emphatic agreement with Plato's intention or method. Though the indication of emphasis is unmistakable in this usage, the identification of the speaker or speakers may be doubtful. "We," whether emphatic or otherwise, usually means Averroes; it is a *pluralis maiestatis*. But "we" or "us" may also mean something like "we moderns" (35.12, 18-19) or "we investigators" (53.19, 29) or "we adherents of the *sharī'a*" (63.3; 66.15) or "us Muslims" (66.22; 81.4) or "us men" (72.8) or "we Andalusians" (66.21; 97.6) or "we Córdobans" (84.22; 96.24). Even this list is not exhaustive. In ruling out any sort of property for the guardians, Averroes considers briefly the possibility that possessing riches may be a virtue. However one decided, that question would have no bearing on the case of the guardians, "for we ourselves do not wish them to be simply virtuous but rather virtuous inasmuch as they are guardians" (42.21-22). Is it farfetched to say that a founder of cities or a teacher of founders speaks here?

Averroes confronts us in another way when, at least seven times, he momentarily puts aside his modest garb as a reporter of what Plato "said" and pronounces a certain problem or topic fit for inquiry or for penetrating investigation. Whether the bringer of the *sharī'a* ought also to be a prophet is a problem of the latter sort. Having stated the problem, Averroes leaves its resolution open, promising to "investigate it in the first part of this science, God willing" (61.17-18). What is not left in doubt is that, for Averroes, the requirements for the Lawgiver are identical with the requirements for the philosopher, namely, mastery of the theoretical and practical sciences as well as perfection of the moral and cogitative virtues (60.22-61.7; 61.11-13). One might well ask: What does prophecy add, or of what does it consist? Earlier passages suggest that prophecy is an instrument by which men are informed of what lies ahead (41.1-2) and of the details concerning "temples, prayers, sacrifices, and offerings." But the prescribing of such details is not exclusively the province of religious Law (47.24-28). Further, by equating the philosopher and the bringer of the *sharī'a* (61.14), Averroes in effect denies that the *sharī'a* has any decisive superiority.

Equally portentous in its implications for Islam is Plato's "opinion" that the Greeks are the people most disposed by nature to receive the human perfections, especially wisdom. This, too, Averroes declares to be a matter in need of penetrating investigation. He immediately brings forth evidence to contest Plato's opinion: in fact individuals disposed to wisdom are by no means limited to Greece, although such individuals are not distributed uniformly or universally. We might say that non-Greek nations are disposed to the several human virtues' being "broadcast and apportioned among them," particularly the nations in the more equable climatic zones (27.1-13). The context of this discussion is a controversy over the virtue of courage and the art of war. Following Aristotle, Averroes holds that the case here is the fairly common one of a virtue serving as a preparation for an art, and of that art in turn serving to perfect or complete the virtue. Plato, on the other hand, holds that war (and hence the virtue on which it depends, courage) exists only on account of necessity (26.19-29). If, then, Plato is correct about the potentiality for virtue among the various non-Greek nations, there is no call for waging a war to bring civilization to them. They, or the adults among them at least, would be fundamentally uneducable. Against this view Averroes —with Aristotle at his side—takes his stand. In so doing, he both supports and alters the Muslim conception of the just war. He now sees that war as depending on the proper natural conditions, instead of being directed against all men. With nations in the moderate climes, "it . . . is not impossible that many of those who have passed the years of youth should receive the virtues to some extent. . . . Could this [degree of virtue] not be established in them, they would be worthy of being either killed or enslaved, and their rank in the city would be that of the dumb brutes" (27.19-23). Where the Koran sees the just war as leading to the conversion of all mankind to the true religion, Averroes views the just war as a mode of bringing wisdom to those who have the natural potentiality for it. With that as his point of departure, it is not surprising that Averroes holds out the possibility or probability that many of the conquered will be condemned to a life of brutishness.

A recurring theme in these pages—the express or implied comparison of "this city" with "these cities"—offers further evidence of Averroes' own views. Though these recurrent terms have more than one meaning in this work, their use by Averroes is generally free of ambiguity. "This city" may mean the timocratic city (82.15, 16) or the oligarchic city (83.10; 93.7) or the democratic city (83.19; 96.1) or the tyrannical city (85.22; 101.10) or the aristocratic city (79.8), but there is no mistaking Averroes' intention in any given case. The sum of such meanings of the demonstrative pronoun is easily surpassed by the number of instances in which "this city" means the city being founded in the *Republic*. Paired with "this city" for purposes of contrast is the term "these cities." "These cities" are all too well known to Averroes, his addressee, and his readers: they are the cities that exist in deed, not in speech; they are "these cities of ours" (84.20).

Only a few of these pairings can be mentioned here, but they should suffice to show how Averroes, with great economy of language, is able to illustrate and support his intention. (*a*) This city has no need for the arts of adjudication and medicine; "under no circumstances has it either judge or physician." What are called adjudication and medicine in this city have only the names in common with the judging and curing practiced in contemporary cities and in the past. Only old-fashioned, Asclepian illnesses and cures are recognized in this city. "They will not make use in this city (and this is in accord with my cogitation) of most cures other than cures for external things such as wounds, dislocations, fractures, and the like." The implications for the chronically ill—whether in body or in soul—are quickly drawn, though with a certain ambiguity as to whether killing or suicide is indicated (37.15-38.18). (*b*) Just as the wants are not autonomous in this city, so the arts that arise to serve those wants are subject to regulation. Averroes notes the alternating scarcity and glut attending a market in disequilibrium. Neither the kinds nor the numbers of artisans in this city will be "of any chance number." Necessary utility is the touchstone that is applied to all production, be it of cloth or bridles or children (43.28-44.7). (*c*) "The women in this city will practice the [same] activities as the men." Averroes brings forth evidence to show that women can hold their own in war. He sees nothing to rule out the possibility "that there be philosophers and rulers among them." A contrast is then drawn between what the Laws or some Laws prescribe regarding the status of women and what an investigation of the animals indicates. From natural history we are led to see how unnatural is the prevailing treatment of human females. "Since women in these cities are not prepared with respect to any of the human virtues, they frequently resemble plants in these cities." By narrowing or nullifying the capabilities of women, men contribute to the further impoverishment of these cities (53.14-54.10). (*d*) In establishing community of property, women, and children, this city does away with the major inducements for people to set themselves apart from the concerns and good of the whole. "It is evident that if all the things in this city" correspond to this arrangement abolishing privacy, "then it will remove envy and hatred from them as well as poverty and the other evils found in these cities." Of the citizens of this city, Averroes says: "They are indeed happy. They are beset by none of the evils besetting the citizens of these cities" (58.1–14). (e) Unlike this city, whose "existence necessitates that those ruling over it be wise, . . . these cities, presently existing, do not receive any advantage from philosophers and the wise" (63.6–8). Indeed, if perchance "a true philosopher grows up in these cities, he is in the position of a man who has come among perilous animals." For the sake of immediate self-preservation, he does well to isolate himself from others; but in doing so he remains in some sense incomplete, for his perfection is attainable "only in this city that we have described in speech" (64.23–27). We may generalize from these examples and say that for Averroes "this city" is "the virtuous city," Plato's city (79.9, 12, 19, 20; 45.3; 52.21; 87.19; 93.31–32). In contrast to it are "these cities," which are "the ignorant cities" or "the erring cities" (52.13–14, 22; 45.11; 79.11–18). In going as far as he does in using "this city" as the rule or measure, Averroes goes very far indeed in judging contemporary practice and even the norms of the *sharī'a* itself by the standards of Plato's philosophic communism.

Averroes is not always so reserved in making such comparisons and judgments. Occasionally he digresses a bit to elaborate on the implications of his analysis. Thus, for example, the transformation of the timocratic man into the oligarchic man is illustrated by a lesson drawn from more or less contemporary history. The dynasty preceding the Almohad in Andalus was known as the Almoravid. "At first they imitated the governance based on the nomos; this was under the first one of [the Almoravids]." But his successors presided over a continuing decay—first timocracy, tinged with oligarchy; then, finally and fatally, a regime devoted to the pleasures. The overthrow of this last was effected "because the governance that opposed it at that time resembled the governance based on the nomos" (92.4-8). These beginnings, however, are not the only similarity between the Almoravids and the Almohads. There are also analogous or nearly analogous patterns in their subsequent decline in laws and morals. "You can make this clear from what—after forty years—has come about among us in the habits and states of those possessing lordship and status" (103.8-10). That the present, Almohad, rule has decayed is suggested by Averroes more than once. But from what level of excellence has it fallen? The several founders of dynasties to whom Averroes alludes in this work appear to have this in common: their rule originally "resembled the governance based on the nomos" or "used to imitate the virtuous governance" (92.7-8; 89.30-31). Their excellence was at best a quasi excellence, though even this would be a great improvement over the baseness that currently prevails. What remains is hardly a vestige: "Only he among them who is virtuous according to the Legal prescriptions remains in an excellent state [of soul]" (103.11). To follow in the ways of the *sharī'a* is to move in the direction of recovering the earlier resemblance or imitation.

Perhaps the most interesting, ambiguous, and provocative of Averroes' speeches are those which present a controversial Platonic teaching. By "controversial" I mean one that runs counter to either generally accepted notions or the prescriptions of the *sharī'a*. A few examples of Averroes' presentations of these unsettling thoughts show his different responses to controversy. (*a*) At times Averroes openly concurs with Plato. The subject of base stories is dealt with at length by Plato, and Averroes emphatically follows in his steps in condemning them. Among the instances of base stories "generally accepted among us," Averroes singles out for censure the custom of saying that God is the cause of good and evil, that angels can miraculously transform themselves, that happiness is to be understood as a reward and suffering as a punishment for men's deeds (30.22–31.25). This entire theme of base stories ought properly to be considered in the larger context of Averroes' discussion of untrue stories as such—that is, representations or imitations—where the reference to Plato is veiled or at least uncertain and where the lessons to be drawn are that fictions are indispensable for ruling and teaching the citizens and that whatever the multitude can learn of the speculative truth through nondemonstrative means—namely persuasive and affective arguments—is, strictly speaking, no knowledge at all (25.14–26.2). (*b*) At other times, Averroes dissents from what he presents as Plato's position. I have referred earlier to Averroes' parting from Plato on the problem of courage and adopting a view he reports as attributed to Aristotle. Some implications of this controversy for the conception of the just war have been touched upon. A further and necessary implication of Plato's position is the rejection of a universal society, a society envisioned in the remark in which tradition has Muhammad say, "I have been sent to the Red and the Black." Averroes can hardly conceal that such universalism does not accord with Plato's opinion; but he is careful to avoid letting this disagreement become an open conflict between philosophy and the *sharī'a* by asserting that the *sharī'a* view, which is "the indubitable truth," is also shared by Aristotle (46.19–21). In siding with Islam against Plato, Averroes appears to retract whatever concessions he has earlier made to Plato's view that all nations are not equally disposed by nature to virtue. A universal society of true believers again appears to be both desirable and possible. Yet that this is not Averroes' last indication of his views on the matter can be seen from his treatment of a related controversy. (*c*) Not all of Plato's controversial statements are acknowledged as such by Averroes. In view of the fact that Averroes sometimes concurs and sometimes dissents, his occasional silences may also be regarded as meaningful. Though Plato's eugenics is notoriously at odds with the *sharī'a* of the Muslims, Averroes manages to discuss "the arrangement of [the guardians'] procreation" in such an exceedingly guarded fashion that we are compelled to say that he is silent about the conflict (54.23–55.27). Shortly thereafter, he appears to accept the notion of a fixed size for this city (56.23), which implies some kind of birth control (56.18–21) or colonization or both. Averroes does in fact speak of "virtuous cities" (97.13; 79.24–25; 57.6), and in that plurality we may discern an alternative to the universal society that would result from a successful war waged against the Red and the Black. In discussing Plato's condemnation of unlimited warfare against enemies of the same stock and place and language, Averroes writes: "These are to be called ones who have gone astray, not unbelievers. What Plato asserts differs from what many Law-givers assert" (59.20–60.5). Averroes leaves the matter by remarking on the difference between what Plato teaches and what Islam, among others, teaches. Averroes does not blur the contradictory statements by asserting the congruence of the Koran's views and Aristotle's; nor, for that matter, does Averroes declare where he himself stands. He remains silent on one of the great points of contention between philosophy and the *sharī'a:* whether racial and linguistic unity ought to prevail over religious diversity.

These examples are only meant to be suggestive of the richness and many-sidedness of Averroes' discussion. It is a work laden with nuances and ambiguities as well as startling assertions. Without a hint of criticism or misgiving, Averroes not only reports Plato's requirement that there be absolute communism of women and children, but then goes on to treat the necessity of that communism as proved (57.4–5). Finally, Averroes himself accepts this communism, along with community of property, concluding that the necessity, propriety, and utility of all this is self-evident

(57.23–58.14). As was stated earlier, the word "we" may well represent different voices. In support of a tentative identification suggested earlier, I now add this evidence. Averroes says that "there is no city that is truly one other than this city that we [*anaḥnū*] are involved in bringing forth" (44.28–29). That this "we" is, or includes, Averroes himself is suggested by the repetition of the last phrase a few lines later: "Hence, this city that we are involved in bringing forth is in itself great in size and possessed of great power notwithstanding that it has, as Plato says, but one thousand warriors" (45.13–14). Our suspicions and impressions are further aroused and perhaps confirmed when, toward the end of his paraphrase, Averroes invites us to cast our thoughts back to "the things that we ourselves were praising when we were attending to the virtuous city" (93.31–32). This sentence happens to be preceded by "He said." The line separating Averroes and Plato is momentarily—but totally—blurred.

In one fashion or another, the question with which this introduction begins is a question for every serious reader of Plato's *Republic:* Of what use is this philosophy to me? Averroes clearly finds that the *Republic* speaks to his own time and to his own situation. Now, whatever that relevance may consist of, it cannot be based on any simple, obvious congruence of Platonic and Koranic teachings. But if, from the fact that Averroes seems to accept the *Republic*'s teaching (at least as far as the practical part of political science is concerned), we hasten to the conclusion that he has thereby effected a complete break with Islam, we would have asserted something undemonstrable in itself and terribly damaging to Averroes. He does, to be sure, accept that philosophic teaching, by and large; but as the earlier examples are meant to show, he uses that teaching critically, selectively.

Perhaps the greatest use he makes of the *Republic* is to understand better the *sharī'a* itself. The Koran contains laws that transcend ordinary human laws—we shall call them the higher part—even as it contains laws that are analogous to ordinary human laws. This latter part, according to Averroes, presents two ways that lead to God: "One of them is through speech, and the other through war." The higher part of the Law, which consists of those regulations and details made known to the adherents of a *sharīʿa* or nomos by a prophet, would appear to lead men to God through silence rather than speech and through peaceful actions rather than war. Whether or not the *Republic* may be helpful in such matters as well (e.g., by helping men understand better what it means to act justly toward one's fellows), there is at least a strong presumption that the *Republic* can help them perceive "the way in which matters are arranged in those Laws belonging to this our divine Law that proceed like the human Laws" (26.16–18).

Of physical coercion, or the war of civilization, we need say little here: it is not the preponderant mode of instruction followed within the virtuous city. How, then, are men led to God by speech? In two ways, Averroes says: either through rhetorical and poetical arguments, or through demonstrative arguments. The former way is used in presenting the theoretical sciences (or rather, certain conclusions reached by those sciences) to the multitude. The elect few, on the other hand, learn these matters in "the true ways." In an apparent reference to Plato, Averroes goes on to say: "In teaching wisdom to the multitude he used the rhetorical and poetical ways because they [sc., the multitude] are in this respect in one of two situations: either they can know them [sc., the speculative truths] through demonstrative arguments, or they will not know them at all. The first [situation] is impossible [for the multitude]. The second is possible—since it is fitting that everyone obtain as much of human perfection as is compatible with what is in his nature to obtain of this and with his preparation for it" (25.14–23). Since it is by no means impossible that the multitude know nothing of the speculative truths, and since it is categorically asserted that they cannot come to know these matters through demonstration, we are left to deduce that whatever the multitude may come to know of these speculative truths through persuasive and affective arguments is, strictly speaking, not knowledge at all, but belief. Such belief may be useful, even indispensable, but it is no more to be confused with knowledge than moral virtue is to be mistaken for intellectual virtue.

If then, knowledge, strictly speaking, or the way to scientific truth, is the preserve of the few, untruth would seem to be the legacy of the many. In a certain respect the young potential guardians and the multitude of citizens are similarly situated. Neither group can digest a demonstrative argument—the one because of the temporary underdevelopment of its members, the other because of its intrinsic nature. Each member of both groups requires an education in "music" (as well as gymnastic), an education that will "represent" or "imitate" a truth that can be known demonstratively, albeit not by him. Such imitations render accessible what otherwise would be inaccessible; but, being imitations, what they convey is not the real thing. Quoting Farabi, Averroes proposes an education in which true happiness "will be imitated by what is believed to be happiness." It is safe to say that, according to this argument, the multitude will never know any better, that their education is, strictly speaking, an education in an untruth (29.9–30.13; 60.7–12). Averroes reports Plato's condemnation of untrue and base stories but says nothing in this context to preclude the use of noble lies. The subsequent discussion (30.22–32.22) is a subtle interplay between reports of Plato's views and expositions of Averroes' own views, culminating in a defense of kingly lying on the grounds that "untrue stories are necessary for the teaching of the citizens. No bringer of a nomos is to be found who does not make use of invented stories, for this is something necessary for the multitude to reach their happiness." Although Averroes reports in this context Plato's view that "lying does not befit God's rulership," he does not preclude the use of invented stories in the *sharīʿa*, or in that part of it that proceeds like the human Laws.

Plato's *Republic* teaches that the best regime will be ruled by philosophers and that human rulers, or rulers simply—that is, all rulers—must lie. No work speaks more cogently or more pertinently on the theme of the lying philosopher than Plato's *Republic*. If Averroes believed that Islam had been or was on the verge of becoming the best regime, there was every reason to consider with all deliberation what Plato had to teach concerning the ruling—and hence lying—philosopher. Alternatively, if Averroes believed that Islam was not the best regime, there was every reason to consider with all deliberation what Plato had to teach concerning the exposed, vulnerable—and hence lying— philosopher (64.23–27). Averroes, like kindred souls before and after him, found utility, relevance, and value in Plato's *Republic* for various reasons. Not the least of these was Plato's truth about lying.

It is fair to say that in deciding to paraphrase the *Republic*, Averroes is asserting that his world—the world defined and governed by the Koran—can profit from Plato's instruction. Plato is the standard—certainly not "these cities," not even the period of early Islam. What now prevails is distinctly second best: the rule of laws and of interpreters of laws, the parceling of political governance to the separate hands of warrior and judge (81.1–8). What might prevail is the true unity of the virtuous city, the city that Plato constructs in speech. But is its actualization a genuine possibility? Or does Plato's city require that very rule of philosophers which only the prior existence of Plato's city can bring about?

> The answer is that it is possible for individuals to grow up with these natural qualities that we have attributed to them—developing, moreover, so as to choose the

general common nomos that not a single nation can help choosing; and besides, their particular Law would not be far from the human Laws; [if these conditions are fulfilled] wisdom would have been completed in their time. This is as matters are in this time of ours and in our Law. If it should happen that the likes of these come to rule for an infinite time, it is possible for this city to come into being. [62.28–63.5]

The human Laws under which the philosophers now live are not very different from the private Laws of the philosophers. The Koran does not preclude the possibility of the rule of philosophers. But that rule or succession of rulers must go on to the end of time before the truly good governance comes into being. It is this chain of circumstances that Averroes holds out as the alternative to Plato's expulsion from the city of all those over ten years of age (78.24–29). It is, however, an alternative fraught with difficulties. Not least of these is that "in this time" men and cities are more easily inclined to good deeds than to good beliefs. Those who have reflected on these matters will know that these men and cities are no better than their beliefs. "The cities that are virtuous in deeds alone are those called aristocratic" (79.1-8). But it is precisely in the realm of intractable beliefs that the most radical transformation needs to be effected. All things considered, Averroes has not exaggerated in declaring that Plato's manner of bringing about the emergence of the best regime is "quickest, easiest, and best."

I conclude that Averroes is—and deserves to be regarded as—the faithful companion of Plato.

Abbreviations and Symbols

Hebr. Üb. Moritz Steinschneider, *Die hebräischen Übersetzungen des Mittelalters und die Juden als Dolmetscher* (Berlin, 1893; reprint ed., Graz: Akademischen Druck- u. Verlaganstalt, 1956).

MPP Ralph Lerner and Muhsin Mahdi (eds.), *Medieval Political Philosophy: A Sourcebook* (New York: Free Press of Glencoe, 1963; Ithaca: Cornell University Press, Agora Paperback Editions, 1972).

Rosenthal E. I. J. Rosenthal (ed. and trans.), *Averroes' Commentary on Plato's "Republic,"* University of Cambridge Oriental Publications, no. 1 (Cambridge: Cambridge University Press, 1956, 1966, 1969).

⌐ ⌐ Readings adopted from MSS other than MS *A*.

[ ] My interpolations.

For full bibliographic information on short-title citations in footnotes, see Appendix III.

Averroes on Plato's *Republic*

THE TEXT

Averroes' [Epitome] of Plato's *Republic* [and] Its Scientific
Arguments, Which Is the Second Part of Political Science

[The First Treatise]

The intention of this treatise is ⌜to abstract⌝ such scientific
arguments attributable to Plato as are contained in the
Republic by eliminating the dialectical arguments from it.
5 We shall be strict in speaking succinctly of all this. Yet on
account of the ordering of teaching, we ought to preface
an introduction in which the [subject of] study is presented
in due order, for Plato set down ⌜this⌝ book only after
[other] books of his on this science. We shall also mention
as well something of the utility of this science, and its
intention and its parts.

We say: This science, known as practical science, differs
essentially from the theoretical sciences. Now this is clear
inasmuch as its subject differs from the subject of each and
10 every one of the theoretical sciences and its principles differ
from their principles. This is because the subject of this
science is volitional things, the doing of which is within our
power, and the principle of these things is will and choice;

21.1 The Hebrew text of Rosenthal's edition begins on page 21.
The numbers in the left-hand margins of the present translation show
the page and line numbers of the Hebrew in Rosenthal's edition. The
numbers in the right-hand margins are the Stephanus numbers of
corresponding passages in Plato's *Republic*.

Epitome] MSS: explanation (or: commentary). It is unlikely that
this is Averroes' heading. He calls this work an epitome at 60.16, below.
Steinschneider discusses the several terms used to distinguish Averroes'
works of commentary; see *Hebr. Üb.*, pp. 52 f.

21.3-4 Averroes opens his epitome of Aristotle's *Physics* in similar
fashion (*Kitāb al-samāʿ al-ṭabīʿī*, p. 2, in *Rasāʾil Ibn Rushd* [Hyderabad,
1365/1946]).

3

just as the principle of natural science is nature and its subject the natural things, and the principle of the divine science is God (may He be exalted!) and its subject the divine things. Furthermore, this science differs from the
15 theoretical sciences in that their end is knowledge alone; if there is anything of action in them it is by accident, as happens in many of the matters that the mathematicians study. Now the end of this science is action alone, even though its parts differ in their proximity to action. For of the general rules [whose account] is supplied by this science,
20 the more general is further removed from action and the less general is nearer, just as in the art of medicine. Hence it is that the physicians call the first part of the art of medicine the scientific part, and the second the practical. That is precisely why this art has been divided into two parts. In the first part the habits and volitional actions and conduct are treated generally, and here is made known
25 their relation to each other and which of these habits is for the sake of the others. In the second part is made known how these habits are established in the souls, which habit is ordered to which other habit so that the resulting action from the intended habit may become as perfect as can be, and which habit hinders which other habit. In general, this part supplies those matters, taken in their generality, that
22. admit of being actualized. | The relation of what is in the first part of this science to the second part corresponds to the relation in the art of medicine of what is in the "Book of Health and Disease" to what is in the "Book of the Preservation of Health and Removal of Disease." The first part of this art is in Aristotle's book known as the *Nicomachea*, and the second in his book known as the *Governance* [*Politics*] and also in this book of Plato's that we intend to explain
5 since Aristotle's book on governance has not yet fallen into our hands. Before we begin a point-by-point explanation of

what is in these arguments [of Plato], we ought to mention
the things pertinent to this part and explained in the first
part that serve as a foundation for what we wish to say here
at the beginning.

We say: It has already been made clear in the first part
10 of this science that the human perfections in general are of
four kinds—theoretical virtues, cogitative virtues, moral
virtues, and [proficiency in the] practical ⌈arts⌉—and that
all these perfections are only for the sake of the theoretical
ones and a preparation for them in the way in which
preparations preceding an end are for the sake of the end.
It also has been made clear there that either it is impossible
for one man to attain all these virtues or, if it is possible, it
15 is improbable, whereas it is as a rule possible that [all these
virtues] be found [separately] among a multitude of individuals. It also appears that no one man's substance can
become realized through any of these virtues unless [a
number of] humans help him and that to acquire his virtue
a man has need of other people. Hence he is political by
nature. This is not something that is needed for human
perfection alone, but [even] for matters necessary for [mere]
life—matters that man in a certain way shares with the
20 animals, such as appropriating food, securing dwelling
places and clothing, and generally anything that man is in
need of because of the appetitive or vital faculties within
him. This arrangement exists for various reasons: [a] because
of an unavoidable necessity (e.g., its being impossible for
an isolated man to secure what he needs by way of food,
housing, and clothing); or [b] because it is the easier way

22.9-12   Aristotle *Nicomachean Ethics* 1. 13. 1103a3-7, 6. 1. 1138b35-
1139a15, 10. 7. 1177a12–b4; Farabi, *Attainment*, 2.4-5, 26.11-19 (*MPP*,
p. 82 n. 6, p. 67).

22.15-21   Aristotle *Nicomachean Ethics* 1. 7. 1097b8-11; Farabi, *Virtuous City*, 53.8-13 (Dieterici tr., p. 84).

(e.g., its being possible for Zayd not to till the soil and sow
25 seeds [beyond his own needs], but if he tills and sows [with
a view to others' needs too] he will live at greater ease); or
[c] because it is the best way, for if a man has chosen an art
since his early youth and has practiced it for a long time,
his performance in that art will be better. That is one of
the causes that led Plato to hold it inappropriate that any
of the citizens engage in more than one art, as we shall state
later on. Hence the employment of a man in more than one
30 art is either altogether impossible or, if possible, not best.
Since it is impossible that the human perfections be attained
other than in different individuals within a given popu-
23. lation, | the individuals of this species are all different in
natural disposition corresponding to the difference in their
perfections. For if each individual among them were
potentially prepared for all human perfections, nature
would have wrought something in vain; for it is absurd
that there be something possible whose realization is
5 impossible. This matter has already been made clear in
natural science. The sense[s too] attest that individual
humans exist with such characteristics. All the more is this
evident in the noble perfections, for not every man is fit to
be a warrior or an orator or a poet, let alone a philosopher.
All this being as we have characterized it, there ought to
exist an association of humans—[an association] perfect in
every species of human perfection and [whose members] are
10 helped to their completion in that the less perfect follows
the fully perfect by way of preparing for his [own] perfection, and the more perfect aids the less by giving him the
principles of his perfection. A case in point is horsemanship
and the art of bridle-making: the art of bridle-making serves
the art of horsemanship as a preparation, and the art of

23.12-15   Aristotle *Nicomachean Ethics* I. 1. 1094a9-15.

horsemanship prescribes for it the best form for the bridle
and how they [sc., the two arts] may associate in a single
15 intention. The various kinds of priority of rank of one art
⌜over⌝ another are discussed in the first part [of political
science]. If, however, such an association does not exist,
the human virtues either will not be attained at all or their
attainment will be defective. In general, the relation of all
these virtues to the parts of this city will be [as] the relation
of the faculties of the soul to the parts of a single soul, so
20 that this city will be wise in its theoretical part through
which it rules over all its parts in the manner in which a
man wise in the rational part rules through it over all the
faculties of the soul—i.e., the part [of the faculties of the
soul that is] linked to reason rules the spirited and appetitive
part in which the moral virtues are to be found. Hence it
[sc., the city] will draw itself toward appropriate objects in
the measure and time judged by intellect. It will also be
25 courageous in [its] spirited part, but at the place and in
the measure and in the time required of it by wisdom, just
as a man will be courageous in [his] spirited part only when
he uses it in the case, time, and measure required by
intellect. It is the same with moderation and with each and
every other virtue. In general, it will possess all the cogitative and moral virtues; and priority of rank within it will
30 correspond to the priority of rank of these virtues. This is
the very justice that Plato investigated in the first book of
this book and explained in the fourth book. It is nothing
more than that every human in the city do the work that is
24. his by nature in the best way that he possibly can. | This is
only conceivable when the parts of the city are in submission
to what theoretical science and those who rule over it decree.
Hence it is evident that this part—i.e., those who possess
the theoretical sciences and the one who rules over them—is
predominant within it. Just as justice in the soul of each

consists in every one of its parts doing only what it has to do
in the appropriate measure and at the appropriate time—
5 this necessarily occurring in the parts of the soul only when
intellect rules over them—so too in the case of the city. You
ought to know that some of these virtues are ascribed to a
city because they are in one of its parts—such as wisdom
and courage—while others are ascribed to it because they
are in all of its parts—such as justice and moderation. This
10 is evident in itself. But whether the virtue of liberality is in
all parts of this city or only in one part of it is something
that we shall investigate later on, because there is room for
inquiry here. If all this is as we have described it (it having
already been made clear in the first part of this science what
these virtues are unqualifiedly), then ⌜three⌝ things remain
15 to be done here for a complete knowledge of them. [*a*] One
of them is understanding the conditions given which any of
these [virtues] can be actualized. For example, it has already
been said what courage is unqualifiedly and that it is something in the soul intermediate between rashness and timidity
—a habit by which a man acts courageously in the appropriate way and in the appropriate measure and time. But
at the moment of one's acting on it, this definition is in
need of particular conditions; otherwise it would be impossible to act [in accord with that definition]. The end of
20 knowledge in this [matter] is only, as Aristotle says, that
one should act, not that he should know. [*b*] The second
concerns how these virtues may be established in the youths'
souls and gradually develop in them, how these [virtues]
may be preserved once they have been completed, and also

24.10-11   For liberality, see 72.24, below, and note thereto.

24.12-13   Aristotle *Nicomachean Ethics* 2. 7. 1107a33–b14, 5. 1129a–
1138b, 6. 7. 1141a9–b8.

24.18-20   Aristotle *Nicomachean Ethics* 2. 2. 1104a5-9, 6. 1106a13-24,
1106b36-1107a2, 9. 1109a20-30, 7. 10. 1152a8-9.

⌐how⌐ the vices may be removed from the souls of the bad. In general, the case here resembles that in the art of medicine, the latter part of which encompasses and makes known how bodies can grow up in health, how one preserves

25 it, and how one removes diseases from them when they have departed from [the condition of] health. Just so is the case here. [c] The third thing is that we should describe which habit and which virtue when joined to some other virtue will make the effect of that virtue more complete, and which habit hinders which other habit. Just as the physician will tell which thing joined to what other thing in the body will

30 lead to health and preserve ⌐it⌐, so is the case here. All this can be understood only by knowing the ends of all these perfections and what is intended through them inasmuch as they are a part of a city, just as the preservation of the health of the organs and their restoration to it is understood for the most part only by knowing their relation to the other organs and their rank among them. |

25. After having made all this clear, we shall state through explanation the way in which each and every virtue comes to exist in the citizens' souls and how to bring this about. You ought to know, besides, that however possible it may be to formulate these in speech, that does not yet suffice to bring them about in deed in cities and nations until such time as the cogitative faculty is joined to it, as is the case in

5 the art of medicine. Hence it is said that the governance of cities is appropriate for the old in whom knowledge of the theoretical sciences is associated with long experience; just as the physician will only be complete when, together with

24.23-25 Aristotle *Nicomachean Ethics* 1. 13. 1102a16-26, 5. 9. 1137a9-17, 10. 9. 1179b29-1180a5; Averroes, *Decisive Treatise*, 22.8-23.14 (*MPP*, pp. 182 f.).

25.2-8 Aristotle *Nicomachean Ethics* 6. 7-8. 1141b8-1142a30, 10. 9. 1180b28-1181b12.

knowledge of the immutable universals of the art, there is
realized in him through experience the cogitative virtue—
[the virtue] through which he can actualize them [sc., the
universals] in matter. All this has been made clear in the
first part of this science; we return, then, to what we were
about.

10   And we say that the virtue of courage is that with which
Plato began to introduce the discussion of the bringing-
about of these virtues. As we have said, the way of understanding how it is attained by the citizens and preserved
with respect to them in the most perfect manner [requires
that] we consider what is primarily intended by the actions
of this virtue in the city. We say that there are two ways by
which the virtues in general are brought about in the souls
15   of political humans. [*a*] One of them is to establish the
opinions in their souls through rhetorical and poetical
arguments. This is limited to theoretical sciences presented
to the multitude of humans, while the way by which the
elect few learn the theoretical sciences are the true ways, as
shall be stated later on. In teaching wisdom to the multitude
he used the rhetorical and poetical ways because they [sc.,
20   the multitude] are in this respect in one of two situations:
either they can know them [sc., the speculative truths]
through demonstrative arguments, or they will not know
them at all. The first [situation] is impossible [for the
multitude]. The second is possible—since it is fitting that
everyone ⌐obtain⌐ as much of human perfection as is
compatible with what is in his nature to obtain of this and
with his preparation for it. Furthermore, their believing
what they endeavor to believe of [what pertains to] knowl-
25   edge of the first principle and of the final cause, as far as it is

25.15 Compare the following discussion (to 26.11) with Farabi,
Attainment, 31.8-33.8, 40.2-41.11 (*MPP*, pp. 71 f., 77 f.); and Averroes,
Decisive Treatise, 15.9-13, 21.4-22 (*MPP*, pp. 176, 181).

in their nature to believe, is useful with regard to the other moral virtues and practical arts, which they were being prepared [to acquire]; and once the moral virtues and practical arts are established in their souls in this first way they can also be led toward performing the actions of these arts and virtues through the two kinds of arguments to-gether, namely persuasive and affective arguments, which
30 will move them toward the [good] qualities. This first way of teaching will mostly be possible only for whichever of the citizens grew up with these things from the time of his
26. youth. Of the two ways of teaching, this one is natural. | [*b*] The second way [of teaching], however, is the way applied to enemies, foes, and him whose way it is not to be aroused to the virtues that are desired of him. This is the way of coercion and of chastisement by blows. It is evident that this way either will not be applied to the members of the virtuous city or, if it is applied, it will be nothing other than
5 the training that is most effective for learning discipline, namely the art of war and military training. As for the other nations, which are not good and whose conduct is not human, why there is no way of teaching them other than this way, namely to coerce them through war to adopt the virtues. That these two ways of teaching the multitude are natural is clear from how the heads of households instill
10 discipline in their children, youths, and servants. Also similar to this is the way followed by those who govern cities that are not good: they castigate their people by means of disgrace, occasional flogging with rods, and execution. But that city which we are describing in speech will minimize the occurrence of this way in it—i.e., discipline secured through coercion. This way, however, will be necessary with

26.1   applied] or: he applies.
26.6   conduct] or: guidance.
26.13-14   See 41.6-7, below.

15 respect to the other nations—those without; in the case of
the coercion of difficult nations, nothing will be without
war. This is the way in which matters are arranged in those
⌜Laws⌝ belonging to this our divine Law ⌜that⌝ proceed
like the human Laws, for the ways ⌜in it⌝ that lead to God
(may He be exalted!) are two: one of them is through
speech, and the other through war. Since this art of war is
20 not completed other than by a moral virtue by which it
draws near to what is appropriate and in the appropriate
time and measure—i.e., the virtue of courage—it is necessary that this virtue be found in virtuous cities as a ⌜prepa-
ration⌝ for this activity. It may be seen from the character
of this virtue that it will not complete its activity unless the
art of war is joined to it, as is the case with many of the
25 moral virtues and practical arts. For it is apparent in many
of the virtues that they are only preparatory for the sake of
the arts, and many of the arts for the sake of the virtues.
This is what Aristotle asserts about the wars of the virtuous
city, according to what Abū Naṣr [al-Fārābī] reports. But

26.14-15 Avicenna, *Metaphysics*, 10. 5 (453.2-7) (*MPP*, p. 108).

26.16 The word "Law," in its capitalized form, is used in this
translation consistently and exclusively to render *tōrah* (= *sharīʿa*). By
his earlier contrast between nations whose governance or conduct is
human and those that are nonhuman (26.6), Averroes in effect identifies human governance with that of the virtuous city, or human Law
with the philosopher's law. It is hard to avoid the conclusion that the
Koran is being praised here for its conformity to the latter. For the
superhuman part of the *sharīʿa*, see 47.24-28, below.

26.19, 23 art of war] MSS: partial art. Reading *al-ḥarbiyyah* for a
presumed *al-juzʾiyyah* in the Arabic. Compare variant reading to Farabi,
Attainment, 25.18, in *Alfarabi's Philosophy of Plato and Aristotle*, p. 154.

26.25-26 Aristotle *Nicomachean Ethics* 1. 1. 1094a1-18; Farabi, *Attainment*, 24.9-26.19 (*MPP*, pp. 66-68).

26.27 There is no positive identification of what work of Farabi is
being referred to here. Pines, p. 75, draws attention to Farabi's enumeration of perfect—i.e., self-sufficient—communities, of which one
type encompasses the entire inhabited earth: *Virtuous City*, 53.8-19
(Dieterici tr., pp. 84 f.). See note to 46.20-21, below.

from what we find concerning this in this book of Plato's, why according to him this part [of the soul, sc., courage] is not prepared for this end [sc., war] but rather is on account of necessity. This is due either [a] to a primary intention of
30 removing from other cities that which they [sc., the members of the virtuous city] detest, namely their ⌜money⌝—and this, either because of necessity or in search of the best—or [b] to a secondary intention in relation to guarding against
27. what might possibly harm the city from without. | This opinion would only be correct if there were but one class of humans disposed to the human perfections and especially to the theoretical ones. It seems that this is the opinion that Plato holds of the Greeks. However, even if we accept that they are the most disposed by nature to receive wisdom, we cannot disregard [the fact] that individuals like these—i.e.,
5 those disposed to wisdom—are frequently to be found. You find this in the land of the Greeks and its vicinity, such as this land of ours, namely Andalus, and Syria and Iraq and Egypt, albeit this existed more frequently in the land of the Greeks. Furthermore, even if we accepted this, we might perhaps say regarding the other virtues that it is not impossible that one kind of nation be ⌜more⌝ disposed by nature with respect to some virtue. The example of this is

27.2-6 Compare Plato 435e-436a. The men of Egypt are there classed among those distinguished for their love of money. In *Attainment*, 38.14-17 (*MPP*, p. 76), Farabi repeats the report that philosophy in ancient times existed among the Chaldeans, moving then from Iraq to the Egyptians and thereafter to the Greeks, from whom the Syrians and finally the Arabs received it. See also Maimonides, *Yemen*, 8.15-16 (Cohen tr., p. iii), for the characterization of the Syrians, Persians, and Greeks as the most expert and learned of the nations; and *Astrology*, 351.13-20 (*MPP*, p. 230), on the follies of the Chaldeans and Egyptians, among others. Averroes is conspicuously silent about the Arabs. See the discussion in Muhsin Mahdi, *Ibn Khaldūn's Philosophy of History* (Chicago: University of Chicago Press, Phœnix Books, 1964), pp. 199-201.

that the part of wisdom is more in the Greeks, and the
10 spirited part in the Kurds and the Jalāliqah. There is room
here for penetrating investigation. It might be thought that
where ⌜the part⌝ characterized by wisdom is most present,
there the virtues are most appropriate and most established
—i.e., established by nature. However one accounts for the
matter, the majority of the kinds of nations are indeed
disposed that these virtues be broadcast and apportioned
among them, and particularly [those in] the two equable
climates—i.e., the fourth and the fifth. It seems one might
say in argument for Plato that it is possible for humans to
15 excel in these virtues only if they have been raised with
them from youth, but if these have been lost to them after
these years have passed, this is no longer possible for them.
If that is so, there is no case here for coercing under a
virtuous governance one who has already come of age and
grown up. But even so, it would be necessary that they be
coerced by taking their children from them ⌜and ordering⌝
them toward the virtues. It also is not impossible that many
of those who have passed the years of youth should receive
20 the virtues to some extent, in particular those who have not
been raised under a governance close to a very virtuous

27.9   The Jalāliqah or Jilliqiyyūn are the warlike and courageous
inhabitants of Jillayqiya, an area that is wider than that covered by
Galicia in Spain, extending from the Duero to the Bay of Biscay and
the Atlantic to Castilla in the East. See Abdurrahman Ali El-Hajji,
"Christian States in Northern Spain during the Umayyad Period,"
Islamic Quarterly, 9 (1965): 47, n. 1.; also, his edition of al-Bakrī, *The
Geography of al-Andalus and Europe* (Beirut, 1968), 71.2-3, and map
opposite p. 64 (Mahdi).

27.10   This is not Averroes' last word. See 46.20-21, below.

27.13   Aristotle *Politics* 7. 7. 1327b23-24; Ibn Ṭufayl, *Ḥayy*, p. 20
(Gauthier tr., p. 18 and n. 4).

27.21-23   Farabi, *Political Regime*, 87.7-17 (*MPP*, p. 42); Avicenna,
Metaphysics, 10. 5 (453.6-9) (*MPP*, p. 108); Ibn Ṭufayl, *Ḥayy*, pp. 147,
153 (*MPP*, pp. 158, 160). See also Maimonides, *Guide*, II 36 (79b)
(Pines tr., p. 372).

governance. Could this [degree of virtue] not be established in them, they would be worthy of being either killed or enslaved, and their rank in the city would be that of the dumb brutes.

After it has become clear from this speech what was intended concerning just wars, it is proper that we 25 proceed with what Plato says about choosing those natures that are disposed with respect to these virtues and about what stratagem should be employed in establishing them in their souls and so accustoming them to them [sc., these virtues] that the actions proceeding from them would be most fully consonant with this virtue. We say that Plato holds that not a single man among the citizens should grow up with more than one art. This is because not every man is 30 fit by nature for more than one art. Further, only by growing up with it from youth does a man acquire the habit 28. by which the ⌐activity⌐ of the art is improved. | Now if a man will not succeed in the tournament game called *tornei* and the sport of horse-racing without persisting in both of them and growing up with them from youth, so ought to be the case in the art of war. Moreover, since many of the arts are being perfected at the same times and ⌐their times⌐ coincide, busying oneself with more than one art will neces- 5 sarily frustrate the actions of them [all]. It is on account of ⌐ all this that Plato asserts that the guardians should be cut 374de off from the other arts. He also holds that in choosing from ⊢ among the [different] natures for this activity, the fitting 375 [candidate] would be one who joins to bodily strength quickness of movement and keenness of sense so that he instantly perceives a thing, runs to inquire into it, and grasps it. It is like the case of the nature of a puppy and of the dog used in hunting, for there is no difference between 10 the two natures as far as what is required of it for guarding.

27.24 Paragraphing supplied.

These, then, are the bodily dispositions that the guardian
and the warrior ought to have. As for the qualities of the
soul, it is required of him that he be ⌐spirited⌐ by nature,
for one who has no spiritedness will be unable to become
heated or to repel. In this matter the case of man is like the
case of the other animals, except that it might be thought
difficult for one formed with these qualities in his body and
15 soul to be able to hate and to love. For two opposite things
ought to be associated together in these people: one of them
is that they have utmost ⌐love⌐ and feeling for the citizens;
and the other, utmost force and grief for their enemies. On
account of this it is thought impossible that a man be formed
by nature with these two dispositions. But the guardian will
not be much of a guardian unless these two dispositions are
20 associated together in him. As for its being thought impossible, why its possibility may be observed in many of
the animals. An example is the dog of strong dispositions,
who is formed with a similar nature. He is one of the most
companionable of things toward one who frolics with him
and the opposite of this toward whomever he does not
recognize.

He says: It is a condition for being a guardian, therefore,
that he by nature love the one whom he knows. This nature ⊢—
25 is, without a doubt, a philosophic nature, for in choosing   376ab
the thing with a view to knowledge and wisdom he is by
nature virtuous. And he will hate whomever he does not
know, not because of some prior harm the other had caused
him, ⌐but⌐ for his very ignorance of him; just as his love for
one whom he knows will not be because of some prior good
the other had caused him but because of his very knowledge
[of him]. The same is the case with the animals to whom we
30 previously compared the guardian. That is, on coming face
to face with a man unknown to him he will hate him even
without there being any prior harm caused him by the

29.   other; | ⌐and on seeing¬ a man known to him he will frolic
       with him even though no good has come from him. Indeed,
       we have made this nature a condition for being a guardian
       in order that he have these two opposite dispositions in
       consummate [form]: love for everyone whom he knows,
       namely the citizens, and hatred toward whomever he does
   5   not know, namely the enemies without. For love or hatred ⊢—
       grounded in advantage and disadvantage would prevent   417b
       this [union of opposites], turning enemies into chiefs and
       chiefs into enemies. This is self-evident. It has, then, been ⊢—
       made clear from all this that the guardians and the fighters 376c
                                                                      376e
       ought to be in their natures philosophers, lovers of knowl-
       edge, haters of ignorance, spirited, quick of movement,
       strong in body, and with keen sense[s]. As for the mode of
       teaching them discipline and bringing them up, that will be
  10   in two ways: one of them ⌐through¬ gymnastic, the second
       music. Gymnastic is for acquiring true virtue for the body,
       and music is for the discipline of the soul and its acquiring
       virtue. This discipline—i.e., discipline through music—is ⊢—
       usually prior in time because the faculty for understanding 377a
       precedes the faculty for exercise. By "music" I mean
       imitative arguments having a ⌐melody¬ from which the
  15   citizens receive discipline. It is only intended that they ⌐
       [sc., the arguments] have a melody because thereby they   └
       become more thoroughly effective and more fully moving to
       the souls. For the art of music, as has been made clear, only
       serves the poetical art ⌐and carries forward¬ its intention.
       The arguments by which the citizens are disciplined are, as
       we have said, either about scientific things or about practi-
       cal things. These arguments are of two kinds: demonstrative
  20   arguments, [and those that are] dialectical, rhetorical, and

29.17-29 Averroes, *Decisive Treatise*, 6.15-21, 15.9-16, 19.10-20.1
(*MPP*, pp. 169, 176, 179 f.); Maimonides, *Guide*, I 33 (36b-37a) (Pines
tr., pp. 70-72).

poetical. The poetical arguments are more particularly for
the youths. If, when they grow up, some one of them is fit
to move on to a [higher] stage of learning, he [sc., the ruler]
brings that about in him, to the point that one of them
arises who has it in his nature to learn the demonstrative
arguments. They are the wise. He who does not have this in
his nature remains at the stage beyond which there is no
possibility in his nature for him to pass. This would be either
at [the stage of] the dialectical arguments or at the two
ways common to the instruction of the multitude, namely
25 the rhetorical and poetical, the poetical being more widely
common and more particularly fit for the youths. The
theoretical things, for the most part, are the concern of all
[students of] divine [science], except for whatever of this it
is thought ought to be imitated as far as possible by ⌈all⌉
men in relation to the completion of their intention and
goal, and particularly the humans of whom we spoke—for
example, as when he [sc., Plato] says of the dead that they
30 are alive in some other manner than the untrue fables
declare. As for the theoretical things which ought to be
imitated to the most exalted degree, why Abū Nasr [al-
Fārābī], in his book "On the Degrees of Being," has spoken
30. of them, and this may be brought over here from there. | As
for the practical matters, they too are matters that have
been made clear in this science. Of the imitations, as he
says, some come close [to the original], some are remote
[from it], some are correct, some untrue. An example of an
untrue one would be if you were to represent a ⌈man's⌉

29.32 Farabi's *Political Regime* opens with a discussion that might
suggest such a title for that work, though it was not known by that
name. The quotation that Averroes reproduces a few lines below is
drawn from Farabi's *Attainment*.

30.2 Farabi, *Political Regime*, 85.6-10, 14-17, 86.11-87.4 (*MPP*, pp.
40 f.); *Virtuous City*, 69.19-70.16 (Dieterici tr., pp. 110-112).

30.3 represent] Same root as "imitate" and "imitation," above.

form by an ox's form. Now these ought not to be used at
all in this city for they are very harmful. Similarly the
5 remote ones ought as far as possible to be rejected. But the
imitations that come close [to the original] are those that
ought to be made here, just as we imitate the first principle
and the second principles "by their likenesses among political principles. The divine acts are imitated by the acts of
the political principles, and the acts of the natural powers
and principles are imitated by their likenesses among the
voluntary powers and arts. The intelligibles among these
are imitated by their likenesses among the sensibles, such as
10 the imitation of matter by privation or ⌜darkness⌝. The
kinds of ultimate happiness—that being the end of the acts
of the human virtues—are imitated by their likenesses
among the goods that are believed to be the end. The
happiness that is truly happiness will be imitated by what
is believed to be happiness. In general, the ranks of the
beings in existence are imitated by their likenesses among
ranks of place and time."

Plato says that what is most harmful for children is that
15 they hear untrue stories during their childhood, for they are
ready at that time easily to accept whatever forms they
wish them to accept. Hence one should guard against their
hearing any of the untrue imitations at this time, and in
general guard the beginning of their upbringing with utmost
watchfulness, for the beginning of every action is very
weighty. And we shall beware, as Plato says, of accustoming
their souls to, and leading them by, base fables even more
than we beware of ⌜the harm to their bodies from snow⌝—
20 this [especially] when we hand them over while they are
⌜yet⌝ small to wet-nurses, who train them. Later, ⌜when

377b-
378e

30.6   second principles] The reference is to the causes or principles
of the heavenly bodies.
30.6-13   Farabi, *Attainment*, 41.1-10 (*MPP*, pp. 77 f.).

they have become strong⌐, they lead them to temples and
houses of sacrifices. But the untrue ⌐and base⌐ stories will
not achieve the purpose. Plato recounts of this what was
generally accepted in his time and warns against it. We ∟
ourselves follow after him and also recount of this what is
generally accepted among us. We say: Among these base
imitations—in accord with what has been explained in the
25 theoretical sciences—is the custom among humans of saying
that God is the cause of good and evil. But He is perfectly
good; He neither does evil at any time whatever nor is the
cause of it. The statement concerning this made by the
Mutakallimūn among the people of our time—[to the effect]
that good and evil are not to be conceived in relation to
God (may He be exalted!), but that ⌐all⌐ actions [in them-
selves] are good—why that is a sophistic statement whose
absurdity is apparent. For by this account neither good nor
evil would have a fixed nature in itself, but would be good
30 or evil by fiat. Evil ought, therefore, to be attributed to
another principle, as this is said of Ashm'day and the
demons, though these imitations too are bad in another
respect. For if a youth hears from the outset that there are

30.26 our time] This phrase may include more than contempo-
raries; often it refers to our epoch, the time of universal, monotheistic
religions, as distinguished from pagan times.

30.27 in themselves] MSS: associated (or: persisting) with Him.
The emendation is made in the light of the fuller discussion in Averroes,
Exposition, 113.13-15 (Mueller tr., p. 104). By this argument of the
dialectical theologians, it would be impossible to blame anything done
by men who are not living under the Law, since the praise or blame
attached to deeds stems solely from the prescriptions of the Law.

30.28 Averroes, *Decisive Treatise*, 24.5-8 (*MPP*, p. 183). See also
Maimonides, *Guide*, I 71, 73-76 (93b-98b, 104b-128a) (Pines tr., pp.
175-184, 194-231), for a systematic presentation and refutation of the
arguments of the Kalām.

30.30 Ashm'day] The chief of the demons. Steinschneider conjectures that Averroes had originally written Iblīs, "the *diábolos* of the
Arabs" (*Hebr. Üb.*, p. 225).

demons that cause walls to tumble upon people, that they
31.   cannot be held fast with locks, that | they see but cannot be
seen, that they exist wherever they wish, that they are
clothed in whatever form they wish, it is certain that he will
not end up a distinguished guardian. For these things will
implant soft-heartedness and fear in the youths' hearts and
establish these in them. Even baser than this is saying of the
angels as well that they can change themselves into different
forms, and this because it is the work of miracles. Hence,
5   evil ought rather to be attributed to the imitation of matter,
as when one attributes evil to darkness or to privation.
Many things belong to the class of those attributing evil to
God; they will not be concealed from one who looks at
them ⌐closely⌐. Also among the imitations that are not good
are imitations of happiness as being a recompense for actions
through which happiness ordinarily is attained and a reward
for renouncing actions through which happiness ordinarily
10   is not attained, and of suffering as punishment for renouncing virtuous actions and clinging to defective actions.
For the virtues that come to pass from such imitations are
closer to being vices than virtues. Hence the moderate one
among them is only moderate regarding pleasure ⌐so as to
obtain an even greater pleasure⌐. Similarly the courageous
one is not courageous because he holds death to be good but
because it is a thing over which fear of an even greater evil
15   takes precedence. Similarly the just one will not refrain

31.7   imitations of happiness] Compare the following passage (to
31.24) with Farabi, *Aphorisms*, 82.10-84.3, 34.6-35.5 (Dunlop tr., pp.
61 f., 33 f.).

31.11-12   Contrast Averroes, *Incoherence*, 585.3-6 (Van den Bergh
tr., 1: 361): " . . . the doctrine of the beyond in our religion . . . is
more conducive to virtuous actions than what is said in others. Thus to
represent the beyond in material images is more appropriate than
purely spiritual representation. . . ." Pines, p. 81, n. 35, suggests that
this passage be considered in the light of the peculiar polemical purposes
of the *Incoherence*.

from the property of humans because he holds this obligatory in itself but leaves it alone so as to attain thereby twice
as much hereafter. Moreover, his movement toward many
of the noble virtues will be for the sake of the base things—
since most of the imitations concerning recompense are only
of sensual pleasures—so that a man would only be courageous, just, faithful, and have virtues predicated of him, in
order that he might copulate, drink, and eat. All this is
20 self-evident to one trained in the sciences. It seems that the
dispositions that come to pass in the soul from these imitations resemble the dispositions that come to pass in those
who restrain themselves—they are not virtues at all. One
ought rather to believe that happiness comes to pass from
the actions that bring it about, in the way in which health
comes to pass from nutriments and medicines. This is
likewise the case with [actions that bring about] suffering,
in the way in which wisdom comes to pass from learning.
Hence, if happiness were represented as the health of the
25 soul, and its immortality and eternal life, that would be a
fitting story.

Plato said: Such guardians as these, if they wish to be of ⌐
utmost strength and courage, ought not to be frightened by   386ab
forewarnings of what might meet them after death. If some
one of them should imagine such things, he would choose to

31.22-24   Averroes, *Decisive Treatise*, 19.2-3 (*MPP*, p. 179).

31.24-25   On religion as representation or similitude, consider the
larger context of Farabi's remarks quoted earlier by Averroes at 30.6-13.
See Farabi, *Attainment*, 40.5-41.12, 44.2-13 (*MPP*, pp. 77 f., 79 f.). Just
as there may be a variety of virtuous nations or cities, so may there be
a variety of virtuous religions (Farabi, *Political Regime*, 85.14-86.10
[*MPP*, pp. 40 f.]; Ibn Ṭufayl, *Ḥayy*, pp. 136, 144 [*MPP*, pp. 153, 157]).

31.26-30   Some light is cast on this passage by the fuller discussion
in Farabi's *Book of Religion* where he distinguishes between opinions and
actions. (1) Opinions may concern (*a*) theoretical matters—among
which Farabi lists a description of death and the afterlife, and accounts
of the happiness and misery attained by men in that afterlife; and
(*b*) volitional things—descriptions of both good and bad rulers and their

be oppressed ⌐and enslaved⌐ rather than to die in war. Such |—

stories as these ⌐ought⌐ to be rejected concerning theoretical 387

30 matters. As for the stories that ought to be rejected con-

32. cerning practical matters, why they are the stories | that

conduce to baseness and defectiveness. So it is necessary that

women's songs be kept from them and that they not hear

them. This is because none of them ought to believe that his

companion's death is something grievously hard for him to

bear, and that in death [his companion] has been overtaken

by an evil because of which he will mourn and weep over

5 him. The opposite ought to be the case with the guardian—

i.e., either he will not be grieved about it at all, no matter

what beloved, companion, or relation is missing; or he will

grieve but little, enduring such sorrow as comes upon him

patiently and well. Weeping, too, is an activity of ⌐women

and⌐ weak souls, very far from the nature of the guardian; |_

hence prophets and chiefs ought not to be characterized as

being fearful.

10   He said: They ought not to be lovers of laughter, for in ⌐

even barely indulging his soul with powerful laughter, a 388e

man will have need of a powerful countermeasure to remove

from that condition. That is why the righteous and the

chiefs ought not to be characterized by excessive laughter.

He said: They ought to be exhorted with exceptional |—

diligence for zeal for the truth, for lying does not befit God's 389

⌐rulership⌐ or the angels or the multitude of humans—i.e.,

15 they ought not [even] to come close to it. So if some artisan

or some other of them be found to be lying, he ought to be

punished. The multitude ought to be told that when one of

followers, their actions, and what they come to. (2) Actions comprise
(*a*) what one does in speech wherein, among other things, rulers are
praised or blamed; and (*b*) estimations of actions and transactions
among people, and defining what is just in these cases (*Alfarabi's Book
of Religion and Related Texts*, ed. Muhsin Mahdi [Beirut, 1968], 44.14-
46.10).

the multitude lies to the chiefs, there is a possibility of harm
resembling the harm that comes when an invalid lies to the
physician about his sickness. But the chiefs' lying to the
multitude will be appropriate for them in the respect in
which a drug is appropriate for a disease. Just as it is only
the physician who prescribes a drug, so is it the king who
20 lies to the multitude concerning affairs of the realm. That is
because untrue stories are necessary for the teaching of the
citizens. No bringer of a nomos is to be found who does not
make use of invented stories, for this is something necessary
for the multitude to reach their happiness. Above all, they
ought to reject statements that conduce to [preoccupation
with the] pleasures. This is prevalent in the poems of the
Arabs. They will listen to statements warning them to shun
them [sc., the pleasures] and against indulging in them, for
25 self-control—as Plato says—can only be [found] together
with moderation and shunning the sensual pleasures, as will
be made clear from his statement in what follows. The
greatest of the acts of self-control is that these people faith-
fully obey the great ones among them and become chiefs
ruling over the pleasures rather than those whom the
pleasures rule. Hence it is inappropriate to decide that they
should listen to statements that incite them to such acts [of
30 self-indulgence]. Hence it is most harmful of all if the great ⊢
ones and the chiefs are described as having even one of ³⁹⁰
these dispositions, and even if only for a brief time. Nor is it
appropriate that they hear statements exhorting them to
33. hold and acquire property, | for more than anything else,
possessions hinder these arts as is said hereafter. The youths
ought to be warned against listening to this and what
resembles it. You know that the poems of the Arabs are ⌞
filled with these evil things. It would therefore be more

32.17-22 Ibn Ṭufayl, *Ḥayy*, pp. 153 f. (*MPP*, pp. 160 f.); Averroes,
Decisive Treatise, 22.8-23.8 (*MPP*, p. 182).

harmful than anything else to accustom youths to them
from the outset. This, then, is the sum of the discussion
5 concerning the class of customary fables.

   Plato does not leave it at letting it be known which fables
ought not to be listened to by the guardians, but also
distinguishes the [manner of] speech they are not permitted.
He says: Narrative statements tell either of past or present
or future things. These stories and legends are one of three   392c–
kinds: either simply a story in which a simple story is told of   394c
10 the thing without imitation, or else a story with an imitation
of the thing being told about. Imitation is of ⌜two⌝ kinds:
either imitation of voice or looks, or imitation through
imitative words. Poetry among the ancients, at first, mostly
imitated through voice and looks. Finally, they fell upon
imitation through words, this imitation being more appropriate for the art of poetry since one imitates through the
15 statement itself, not through something external. The Arab
poets mostly make use of imitations of the latter class—i.e.,
imitation through words.

   After Plato explained the kinds of narrative statements
and explained that they are of two kinds—one, statements
without imitations; the other, statements wherein the thing
being told about is imitated through looks, these being the
most powerful imitations for them [sc., the Greeks]—he then
20 investigated whether or not these guardians ought to imitate, and if so, what are the bounds of the permissible   394e
imitations. He explained that they ought not to be permitted to imitate, for—as has been said—in this city each
and every human turns ⌜only⌝ to one activity that he may
thereby be more prepared for it and better at it. The same
holds for imitations: i.e., if we wish that a man be a good
25 imitator, he should do well at one kind of imitation. Hence   395

   33.23 Literally: The statement concerning imitations is this very
statement.

we find that the nature of some humans is such that they surpass at imitations consisting in blame while others ⌐only⌐ do well at praise (as is said of Ibn al-Taḥam, that he could praise, but not blame). This being so, as they ought not to be permitted to imitate everything, there is no need for them to engage in even one kind of imitation. But as they undoubtedly choose to imitate something, they should—from
30 their youth—imitate what is becoming to them, patterning themselves after those who possess strength, a sound mind,
34. freedom, and other such dispositions. | But they ought not to approach the imitations of the base and vicious because the prolonged continuance of imitations dating back to youth will establish a disposition and nature in both body and soul. That is why he said that the most highly regarded of people ought not to imitate the actions of women crying
5 out in their throes of birth, or women copulating with their husbands, or women—⌐believing themselves already⌐ fit for rulership—quarreling with their husbands, or women mourning, crying, and lamenting. Nor will they be per- ⊢ mitted to pattern themselves after handmaidens and slaves, 396 nor imitate drunkards or madmen. Nor is this all: we will not leave them to imitating the craft of tanners or shoemakers or other such crafts, for just as it is not permitted
10 them to practice these crafts, so is it not permitted them to imitate them. Even less suitable would be permitting them to imitate the prancing of horses, the braying of asses, the

33.25-26 The distinction between imitations that consist in blame and those that consist in praise corresponds to the comedy and tragedy mentioned in Plato 395a. Consider Farabi's discussion: "In tragedy good things are mentioned, praiseworthy matters which are an example for others to emulate. . . . In comedy evil things are mentioned, personal satires, blameworthy characteristics, and reprehensible habits" (Arthur J. Arberry, "Fārābī's Canons of Poetry," *Rivista degli Studi Orientali*, 17 [1937]: 269.16-17, 21-22 [Arberry tr., pp. 275 f.]). The MS versions of this poet's name are corrupt, making his identification uncertain.

sound of rivers and the sound of the sea and the sound of
thunder, for all this resembles madness.   ⌐

    I say: There ought to be rejected the poems that follow
the ⌐Arabian⌐ custom of describing these things and their
15 imitations that come close to being of this kind. Because of
all this, poets in this city ought not to be permitted to
imitate everything. And this on various grounds: [a] The
activity of a given imitator will be good only if one [restricts
one's] imitation to one kind, as in the case of the arts. [b]
Moreover, the imitation of base things or of what has no
bearing on whether something is to be chosen or shunned
(as is the case with many of the poems of the Arabs), is
something for which there is no need in this city. Rather,
the poets in this city ⌐ought⌐ only to be permitted to
20 describe illustrious women and their probity, and, in general, the moral virtues. Just as the poets in this city ought
not to be permitted to imitate any chance thing whatever,
so also is the case with painters. They ought not to paint in   ⌐
this city, and in particular whichever of them paints the   401bc
vicious. As for the virtuous, there is need that the children
25 and the youths should [not only] hear good speeches but
[also] see good things so that beautiful actions be established
in them in every respect. In a similar relation is one who
dwells in a healthy place, receiving benefit from everything
that is brought forth there by way of sweet savors, herbs,
and the like.   ⌐

    This, then, in sum is what Plato says about the fables
through which the guardians are to be trained. After this   ⌐
he lets it be known which class of melodies ought to be used   398c–
30 with these fables in teaching them. As has been said, a   398e
melody occurring in a narrative is composed of three things:
rhythm, harmonic mode, and the speech to which the

34.12   the sea] Following Plato 396b; MSS: song.

melody is set. As for the statements to which ⌐melodies⌐ are
35.   composed, | it has already been stated of what character
they are to be. What remains to be discussed is what he says
as to which of the melodies and which of the rhythms are
appropriate for these. Plato asserts that the melodies making
use of fear and fright will not be suitable for them, just as
speaking without a melody about this class [of fear-inducing
things] will not be suitable for them. Nor will these be
5   appropriate: the soft modes used at a drinking party and
weddings, and in general melodies with many changes, for
these people are not idlers. Only two kinds of modes need ⊢—
to be composed ⌐with respect to them⌐: first, the kind that   399
conduces ⌐the soul to courage and perseverance in wars;
second, the kind that conduces⌐ the soul to whichever of
the virtues he intends for it to accept with ease, calmness,
10   and quietness. The determination of what these composi-
tions ⌐are⌐ belongs to the art of practical music.

Plato, however, defines them by ascribing them to people
generally known in his time for the making of melodies.
This teaching has decayed ⌐in this time of ours⌐. Hence
there ought not to be left in the city any of the instruments
still in use, such as the instrument called the tambourine
and many other instruments. Plato commanded that the
only instruments to be left in the city are those called the
lyre and the cither.

15   He said: And for the country folk a sort of pipe. This also
will be the case with the rhythms. We ought to choose from
among them the kind that is not ordinarily among women
or idlers, but rather the kind that makes for courage of the

35.15   a sort of pipe] The MSS have "customs," probably because
of a mistaking of *al-siyar* for *al-sabz* (i.e., *al-surnāy*), a small flute with a
wide mouth. (In written Arabic, the difference between these two words
is slight.) The instrument is mentioned and illustrated in Farabi's
Kitāb al-mūsīqā al-kabīr, ed. Gh. A. Khashabah (Cairo, 1967), p. 787,
n. 3, and illustration on p. 788 (Mahdi).

soul and an easy conjoining with whatever is desired to be
joined to it. These rhythms were generally known in Plato's ⌞
time, but in this time of ours we ought to investigate them.

20 Plato asserts that when those are chosen in whose nature ⌐
there is a possibility of accepting these virtues and who   402
moreover are brought up in this musical upbringing, they
will reach the utmost in self-control, courage, strength of
soul, love of ⌐beautiful⌐ excellent things, and [in] their
desire ⌐for justice⌐ in both small forms [and large], and in
shunning pleasure. For there is nothing at all in common
between a sound mind and pleasure. That is because pleas-

25 ure throws a ⌐sharp-⌐minded man into a perplexity resembling a madman's, all the more when he goes to excess.
For example, the pleasure of copulation, more than any-   ⊢
thing else, will drive a man mad. Hence ⌐pleasure⌐ should 403a-
                                                          403c
not be mixed with the desire of the musical one; rather he
should desire ⌐only the beautiful⌐ with self-control. But
pleasure has something in common with baseness of soul

36. and the other vices. | This being so, it is improper for the
desirer and the desired—if the one is to desire rightly and
the other is to be desired especially—that their desire turn
to pleasure or have anything in common with it. Hence a
nomos ought to be laid down in this city that love and desire
between them be like the love that is between fathers and
sons. This is the end at which the activity ⌐of music⌐ aims. ⌞

5 This, then, is the sum of what Plato mentions here concerning the subject of music. After this he takes up mentioning gymnastic, food, and in general the things through
which true virtue is acquired—not that this is unqualified
true virtue, as Galen and other physicians say of this, but
that this is true virtue through which is realized that virtue
of the soul which is designed for the activity of guarding,

10 namely the virtue of courage. Gauged in this respect,   ⌐
gymnastic and food not only acquire health for the body, 410b-
                                                          412a

but also acquire ⌜virtue⌝ for the soul in the purpose that has been designated for it. An example is simple gymnastic, which acquires health for the body but also moves the spirited part of the soul and renders it stronger than it had been. Hence Plato commands that we not deal insufficiently with these [guardians] by using gymnastic without music or

15 music without gymnastic. This is because using music by itself renders the soul soft and lax in the utmost quietness and calmness, particularly when one makes use of its soft kinds. Gymnastic, too, by itself renders the soul savage to the utmost degree, impervious to persuasive arguments, becoming rather an extreme misologist, as we see happening in fighters of ⌜gross⌝ disposition and in the undisciplined.

20 Hence these two arts, as Plato says, work on the spirited kind and the philosophic kind of the parts of the soul so that the virtue intended for guardianship is prepared ⌜from their mixture⌝. That is to say, he will bear the utmost ⌞ delight and love toward citizens, and strength toward those without.

He said: The gymnastic that they ought to practice is the ⌜
25 simple, straightforward gymnastic suitable for war. As for ⁴⁰⁴ food, we ought to restrict them to simple foods that combine easy availability with a strengthening of their bodies for what is desired of them, such as roasted meat and simple beets cooked with water, salt, and oil. If they grow accustomed to meals other than this and miss them while in camp, they will fall gravely ill. Hence these ought not to become so habituated in their gymnastic, meal, drink, and passions of

30 their soul, that if they are separated from them it would be a cause of their falling ill. For these people, as Plato says, need health just as a dog has need of keen sight and

37. hearing | more than anything else. Hence they ought not to get drunk, for of [all] human beings the guardian least of all and last of all should get drunk. Otherwise the guardian

would need a guardian. All this being so, drunkenness and
5 meals of varying types are forbidden to the members of this
city; similarly, sweets and whatever resembles them in kind.
In general, their way with food and gymnastic resembles
their way with music, namely that they only make use of
these simple kinds alone. That is because music that is not
simple produces evils in the soul, while gymnastic that is not
simple produces illness in both body and soul. The absence ├──
of discipline in music and unrestrained gluttony in food and ⁴⁰⁵
10 drink, if they increase in the city, will of necessity bring with
them the need for two arts—the art of adjudication and the
art of medicine. Nothing is more indicative of the citizens'
evil dispositions and the baseness of their thoughts than
⌐their being in need⌐ of judges and physicians. This is
because these [citizens] have no virtue at all of their own,
but ⌐only⌐ attain it through compulsion. The greater the
body's need for these two arts and the more they heap
honors on them, the further they are from what is right.
15 Hence, among the properties of this city is that it has no
need for these two arts and that under no circumstances has
it either judge or physician. If there be such, it is [only]
homonymous with the medicine and adjudication performed in cities today. For if the food for these is gauged
with respect to quantity, benefit, time, and [as being of]
good quality, and their movement is of this character, it
seems that they will have no need for many of the cures
20 made in this time of ours and in the past. Plato thinks that
these illnesses, originating in these cities, are new, not
having been matters of watchful concern to the sect of
Asclepius, and that these words by which they are designated are also new—i.e., these illnesses whose cause is a bad └─
mixture of matter, such as abscesses, fevers, and so on. All

37.10-14 Avempace, *Governance*, 8.6-9.5 (*MPP*, p. 126).

this being as we have characterized it, they will not make
use in this city (and this is in accord with my cogitation) of
most cures other than ⌐cures for¬ external ⌐things¬ such as
25 wounds, dislocations, fractures, and the like. They will have ⌐
need there of a physician to distinguish one in whom there   407de
has appeared a defect that can be cured from one in whom   409e–
there has appeared a chronic defect that cannot be cured.   410a
The former will be cured; the latter will be let come to
grief, even if it were possible to keep him alive through
medicines but [at the cost of] his no longer participating in
any of the city's affairs. This, then, is what Plato asserts
30 about the defective ones: namely that there is no need to
cure anyone for whom it is impossible that he truly have all
the virtues. This is because with the disappearance of a   ⌐_
being's end, for the sake of which it was brought into being,
38.   there is no [longer any] difference between | its nonexistence
and its existence. Hence Socrates chose death over life when
he saw that it was impossible ⌐for him¬ to live a human life.
And since every one of the people was only brought into   ⌐
being that he might live as a part of this city so that he   406c–
undertake some action for it, with the disappearance of this   406e
5 usefulness from him, death is better for him than life. Hence
the physicians try to sever from the body any limb that is
already rotting and whose efficacy has been rendered nuga-
tory, such as rotting fingers and ⌐rotting¬ molars. ⌐More-
over¬, if we leave such as these in the city they will com-
monly be a cause for the birth of [additional] defectives.
You can make this clear by considering craftsmen bent on
their work. When they fall sick they ask the physicians to
purge them with an emetic or vomiting or blood-letting
10 that they might thereby return quickly to their work. If he
prescribes this, they obey his orders. But if he orders a

38.1-2   Farabi, *Plato*, 19.3-7 (Mahdi tr., p. 64).

regimen for them that suspends their activity for a long
while, they reject what he says as if they reckoned their
lives to be useless if they are unable to perform through
them those actions that they ordinarily perform. The only ⌞
ones eager for life notwithstanding a chronic defect are
those who loiter at street corners; they are idlers. As for
the defectives for whom it is possible to live without being
15 cured but who cannot possibly further the existence of the
city in any way: some humans [hold that] they ought to be
killed; some humans assert that they ought to be spared.
As for the assertion of those who would place the ⌜burden⌝
[of caring] for them upon the citizens—it is of no account.
This, then, is what leads to the need for a physician in this
city: i.e., that he cure external injuries and distinguish
chronic defects from those that are not chronic. It might
⌜be thought⌝ that there also will be need for him in this
20 city for another matter: namely gauging food with respect
to time, amount, and condition for each and every individual, time, and place. This is done through the cogitative
faculty, which he acquires through experience. Hence the ⌜
physician will not be of this character until—[over and   408de
beyond] his study of the art of medicine—he has encountered
many of the illnesses and experienced this in others and in
himself. By experiencing illnesses in himself he acquires for
himself a knowledge that he could not acquire by perceiving
25 them in others. A judge too will be needed in this city to ⊢
consider whoever has a bad nature and does not accept the 409–
cure—i.e., reproof of the soul; him he will have killed. As 410a
for the one who possibly can accept discipline, him he will
castigate. His knowledge of this will come only after long
experience, because knowledge of the causes of wrongdoing
only comes to him after he has investigated them in others.

38.14-17   Compare Avicenna, *Metaphysics*, 10. 4 (447.12-18) (*MPP*,
p. 104).

It is one of his prerequisites that his soul be not bad but
virtuous from the outset, having grown up on simple music.
30 His case is not like the case of the physician, for the physician is not harmed if he is sick in body. But the judge
cannot possibly be an upright judge if his soul is bad, for a
39. bad soul | knows neither virtue nor itself. Virtue, however,
knows itself and the badness in others through long experience. Hence it is laid down as a condition for a judge
that he must undoubtedly ⌐be⌐ old, for youths know only
the good—that is, youths who have been brought up on
simple music and good fables. It is in this manner, then,
5 that the art of adjudication and the art of medicine exist in
this city.

Further, after this he states the criteria for choosing the ⊢—
nature of that one who is desired as head of these guardians. 412c–
He said: There ought to be chosen that one among them 414a
who is most virtuous and who most loves the advantage of
the citizens and who is most disciplined. This will be only if
various conditions are combined in him, among them that
10 he not depart from this opinion against his will. This is to be
understood in various respects, among them that he will be
moved from it by compulsion (as when beset by sorrow and
fear), and by deception and falsehood (as when being
deceived by one of the appetites or forgetting over time).
This is because there are two kinds of opinion. In one kind,
a man departs from his belief willingly—⌐this is false
opinion—just as shunning evil can be only through his
willing so. In the other kind, a man departs from his belief⌐
against his will—this is correct opinion—just as the good is
taken away from a man other than through his willing so.
15 This will be through compulsion, as we have said, be it by
force or deception or falsehood. Hence one ought to beware
of these changes in him whom one would have neither forget

38.31 upright] Other MSS: expert.

what he is led to believe concerning the obligation of doing
whatever is most advantageous for the city nor ever be
deceived about it. And they should also be tried in things
whereby something of this opinion might be generated in
them—i.e., pleasure—and similarly they should be meas-
20 ured [by means of] terrors. Whichever of them is perfect in
all these dispositions, is not to be moved from his opinion,
standing up to ⌜the test⌝ like gold refined in fire—why this
is the one who ought to be ruling over the city, and he ought
to guard it; and he should be honored in his life and death
and burial and in the other ways by which the living seeks
to commemorate the dead.

Now we shall explain the other conditions that ought
25 to be made for the chiefs—namely the moral and theoretical virtues. For the chiefs in this city are undoubtedly
the wise in whom are combined, along with wisdom,
these virtues and others [as well], in accord with what
we shall recount of this in what is to come. Since it is
possible for one born in the class of guardians not to be
disposed by nature to be a guardian—even though this will
happen infrequently—it also is possible that one born in
40. one | of the classes of citizens other than that of the
guardians be fit to be a guardian—though this too is rare.
That is because each ⌜class⌝ will copulate only within its
own class—i.e., the guardians will copulate within the class
⌜of guardians⌝, and similarly farmers, for example, within
the class of farmers. These being formed by nature for the
activity in which they ordinarily engage, their children's
5 nature will usually be of that nature since father and mother
usually transmit only what resembles the substance of the
two of them. But since, as we have said, this [generation of

39.18-19 Literally: and similarly they should tell of terrifying
things.
39.24 Paragraphing supplied.

like by like] may be thrown into confusion, and since the
thing that ⌜most⌝ leads to—and is the most powerful of
causes of—the destruction of ⌜this⌝ city is that someone
carries on an activity in it to which he is not disposed by
nature, Plato ⌜cleverly provided⌝ that a story be adopted in
10 the city by which the guardians and the rest of the multitude
may be persuaded to transfer their offspring from class to
class. The story is this. We shall say ⌜to them: You⌝ are the ⌜
chosen and the exalted. You were generated in the womb 414de
of the earth with this disposition of yours, your weapons,
and the rest of this before you were completed. When you
were completed the earth brought you forth. ⌜She⌝ is a
mother to you, and you are brothers. Your opinion concerning this is a foundation of the city, an opinion—if
anyone makes war against it—of one who has great feeling
for his brethren born of one earth and one mother. You as
15 a whole are a community of classes of citizens, brothers in ⊢—
that she was your mother. But when God created you, He 415
had in view whichever of you would be fit ⌜to be chief⌝ and
mixed refined gold in His bringing him into being; that is
why they are most honored. He also had auxiliaries in view
and mixed silver in their being. He also considered the poor
and the other working craftsmen and mixed iron in the
20 being of some of them and bronze in others. Since you have
all been generated—notwithstanding that you are of one
class—you are of different kinds. For the most part, an
offspring born to each of you will resemble him in kind.
Sometimes [however] silver will be born of gold, and gold
of silver, and similarly with each and every kind in accord
with this analogy—i.e., that gold or silver will be born of
bronze, and the reverse. Hence God commanded the chiefs
25 that in nothing should they take ⌜such⌝ care in guarding as
in their care in guarding their children, directing their
natures, and examining what is mixed in them. If the son is

bronze they will not ⌐leave him in the midst of the other children⌐ but rather admonish him with coercion in accord with what is due his nature and thereafter thrust him out among the craftsmen and the poor. If it should also happen that these [latter] generate gold or silver, they will honor them and appoint the one who is suitable and appropriate

41.   to rulership. And it is due to his care [for the city] that | the prophet announced that the ruin of this city will only come to pass when its chief ⌐who guards⌐ it is of iron or bronze. This story will be transmitted to them through music from youth, just as the other stories are transmitted to them.

5   When he finished this he said that the settlements of these chiefs and guardians of the city ought to be raised above the city and that if there is one of them who does not wish to accept the Law he will be smitten, and also so that if an enemy from without approaches the city they will attempt to seek him out, pursue him, and avenge themselves upon him. When he had set the bounds of their dwelling places he investigated whether guardians ought to possess anything

10   by which they might be singled out from the citizens by way of their dwellings or otherwise. He said: There is nothing ⊢— more ugly in shepherds than that the dogs they have reared ⁴¹⁶ with a view to guarding whatever they wish them to, should depart from that disposition on account of their hunger or their fear ⌐or some other bad⌐ habitude [and go on] to harm the sheep and to injure them, thus turning into the opposite of [watch-] dogs—⌐wolves⌐. So is it with the guardians: namely that it is among the most injurious of things that

---

41.1   prophet] Plato 415c: oracle.

41.6-7   The virtuous city too has a *sharīʿa* (see also 44.23), which men can be and are compelled to obey. But for Plato wisdom, unlike obedience, is not a product of compulsion (25.17; 26.1-15). A Muslim believer in the war of civilization presupposes the coincidence of wisdom and the *sharīʿa*: by being compelled to obey the Law, men are brought to genuine wisdom.

15 ⌜they have⌝ a disposition that necessarily leads to injury to
the citizens, especially since they are more powerful and
stronger than the other citizens. Of this, then, above all
other things, ought one to be wary in the mighty. (You can
make this clear from the cases of the mighty taken from
these cities, for on the death of the tyrant who had been
subduing them, they turned on the grazing [flock] and
20 devoured them.) Of this matter concerning the guardians,
above all other things, ought we to be wary: namely that
there be in them a disposition by which they leave off being
good guardians [or], even more, cease being guardians
altogether. It is easy to show that none of them ought to
have any possession, neither dwelling nor tools nor anything
else. But they will have a claim ⌜against⌝ the other citizens
25 for what will suffice them for food and clothing. Of gold and
silver they have no need at all. Rather we shall tell them:
You have in your souls something of ⌜a divine⌝ [sort of] this
[sc., gold], which God has given in its place. Because of this,
there is no need of that [sc., gold] from which there arise
damages to others. You are not allowed to mix the virtuous
gold that was given to you with the gold of mortals, for the
money of [such] people is employed in many illicit pursuits
[while] the gold in you is pure, refined gold. You cannot ⊢
42. handle gold | or silver, or store them up beneath the rafters ⁴¹⁷
of the houses, nor seek after them, nor drink in vessels of
silver ⌜or⌝ gold. The acquisition of property is harmful to
the guardians because if they acquire land and houses and
money, each will appropriate for himself and want to isolate

41.17 the mighty] *ha-taqīfīm*. This also implies irascible, merciless.
41.20 The following passage (to 42.2) should be compared with
Plato 416b–417a for several discrepancies, among which are the absence
from Averroes' text of Plato's explicit references to education, the
provision against any locked doors, and the requirement of common
messes. Averroes furthermore converts Socrates' indirect speech into a
direct address to the guardians.

5 himself from the citizens by assembling as much property as
   is possible for him. They will thereby turn into enemies of
   the citizens, haters of them; similarly, one with another. ⌊
   For the most part they will not kill, except for their [own]
   wealth—not for the sake of the citizens. In general, what
   will happen to them in their relations with the citizens and
   with one another—enmity, hatred, and mutual fraud—is
   like what happens to the inhabitants of these cities. Sometimes this is a cause of their conspiring against the citizens
10 and devouring them. In general, citizens will have for them
   the status of enemies, and they [sc., the guardians] fear
   them [sc., the citizens] just as they fear the enemies without
   —and their war will be with them. Or they [sc., the guard-
   ians] may wage an occasional [external] war—but for the
   sake of their [own] lives and wealth. If an enemy harms
   them and they are able to rescue the citizens, they [sc., the
   guardians corrupted by private wealth] will do so and
   especially if they have imposed a tribute upon them by
15 plundering the citizens. Possessions, too, hinder them from
   the business of guardianship. If they ⌜wage war on account
   of their possessions⌝ their guardianship of the citizens will
   be incidental; they will fight when possessions require it of
   them and flee from war when that is not their expectation.
   This is something that necessarily happens to them when
   they are propertied. Because of all this, if we wish the
20 guardians to be in the best condition as guardians, it is
   obligatory that they have nothing at all. Even if the posses-

   42.11-12 Plato 417b: property-holding guardians fear the enemies
   within far more than those without. Averroes goes on to elaborate upon
   what is treated very briefly in the *Republic*.
   42.19-23 Speaking emphatically in his own name, Averroes forbids
   the guardians to own property. This principle is extended to all classes
   of the city in 43.1-14 and reiterated in 60.7-12, and forms the basis
   of his just-completed condemnation of "these cities" in 41.17-24,
   42.7-10.

sion of wealth and riches were a virtue, it would not be
obligatory for guardians as guardians that they be rich.
For we ourselves do not wish them to be simply virtuous but
rather virtuous inasmuch as they are guardians. Imagine
someone saying: You have forbidden these people the most ⌜
25 exalted thing by making them auxiliaries—[making them],   419–
just as Plato said, paupers possessing nothing. This is like   420
someone's saying to one who has drawn a man's form: You
have not put the noblest color on the noblest part, for you
are obliged to paint the eyes—since they are the noblest
part—with the noblest of colors, which is purple, not black.
This is silly, for it is not fit that the appearance of the eye
be fair simply, but rather in respect of ⌜the activity of the
30 eye that comes to pass from it. The case with guardians ⊢
is similar: it is not fit that we seek for them the simply   421bc
exalted thing, but rather in respect of⌝ their being guardians
—assuming that wealth is a virtue. |

43.   When it became clear to him, with respect to the guard- ⊢
ians, that they ought not to possess anything, he also   421de
considered the case of the artisans and workers among the
members of this city. Ought we to permit them possessions
so that they receive wages for their work and [consequently]
have possessions from it? He found this case identical with
the other, since it was clear to him that nothing is more
5 harmful to this city than the entry of poverty and wealth.
For if we permit the artisans to acquire possessions through
their work, the end of their work will be acquisition and
the return they get from the [proper] arrangement of their
wealth. Their usefulness to the citizens will be a kind of
accident, their work being not for the sake of what results
[from it essentially] but rather for the sake of their possessions. This being so, they frequently become confused about

43.6 Essentially, as distinguished from the accidental benefit, viz.,
money.

the end that is truly the end—namely usefulness to the citizens. For if they have a sufficiency, they ⌐detest¬ their
10 work so that they shun it or become idle artisans. If [on the other hand] they are needy, the tools and everything needed for it [sc., their craft] will be too dear for them, and their work will be shoddy. This being as we have characterized it, ∟ it can be seen that Plato asserts that there is no wealth in this city for anyone in particular to acquire and to use as he wishes. This being the case, they have no transactions in gold or silver, nor will they need them at all in this city.
15 For gold and silver, as has been explained in the *Nicomachea*, are only needed in these cities because of the difficulty of transactions; and they also serve as an intermediary between diverse things so that there may be an equality in transactions involving things wherein it is difficult to gauge the existence of equality. A case of the difficulty of transactions: for example, a farmer who wishes to have an iron plow has nothing to give a smith in exchange other than
20 food. But if the smith has no need of food but rather has need of clothing, for example, or something else, their transactions cannot be completed. They need to set up something that is potentially all things, so that when a farmer gives it to a smith and takes an iron plow from him, the smith has already taken all that he wishes for and has need òf. Similarly with each and every one of the other citizens. When the farmers have what is needed by them and the citizens, they gather the food; and the smiths make
25 whatever tools are needed by the citizen; and similarly the weavers, builders, and the others. There will be a kind of money in the city with which all these tools and provisions will be paid for. Then they distribute them among the citizens in the measure that each kind has need of. This is

43.15-17   Aristotle *Nicomachean Ethics* 5. 5. 1133a19-b28.
43.24   make] MSS: take.

with respect to the necessary arts in particular, not to the
unnecessary arts wherein the sole intention is pleasure, such
as the art of the perfumer, the painter, the sculptor, ⌜the
30 maker of ringstones⌝, and other such things in these cities.
It is evident that they will have no need at all of dinar or
dirham. Nor will the numbers of artisans in this city be of
any chance number, so that at one time things will be scarce
44. and at another time | be in a glut, with the arts consequently
being useless, as we see happening with barbers and others
in these cities. Where the art has some necessary utility for
all citizens, they will take a sufficient number of artisans
for it, such as the art of farming and weaving. And where
the art has some necessity only for some class of people,
5 they will also take a [proportionate] number of artisans for
it, such as the art of bridle-making. Hence none of the
members of this city will copulate when he so desires or
with whom he so desires, but rather in a fixed measure so
as to preserve that class whose [determined] number is
intended in the city, as shall be stated hereafter when we
speak of the guardians' copulations.

   After it became clear to him that this city would not ⌐
10 make use of gold or silver, a doubt seized him concerning 422
war with other cities whose lord is wealthy and powerful.
He says: Perhaps it will be too weak to kill the likes of these.
When he considered the matter it became clear to him that
the case is the opposite of what is thought. For wealth and
prosperity cause their possessors to be contumacious, leading
them to neglect the study and drill of war. But when these
guardians grow up in the manner we have stated and attain
15 the martial quality, being also disposed by nature to this,
their standing among the wealthy and prosperous is that of
the wolf ⌜among⌝ the fattened flock. It is possible for these
to battle with twice or thrice their number. (You can see
this clearly in communities that grow up in the desert,

[these people] being [both] tough and poor. They quickly subdue communities that are at ease and prosperous, as happened to the king of the Arabs with the king of Persia.)

20 Also, when this city wages war with another, it must wage war with either two cities or one. If it wages war with two cities, the case here is very easy. For if they rush ⌐their envoy⌐ to one of those two cities with supplication and entreaty, saying to them—"We ourselves make use of neither gold nor silver, for this is not permitted us by our Law, but it is permitted you. Rise ⌐and wage war⌐ together with us so that we take ⌐away their⌐ property and their posses-

25 sions"—if they do this they quickly will be friends with whatever nation they deal with ⌐in this way⌐. Someone might say: Perhaps the members of that city to whom dominion has been given, once they have attained prosperity and filled their hands with loot, will thereby be able to wage war against this poor city. But the case is not as it might seem, for there is no city that is truly one other than

45. this city that we are involved in bringing forth. | The rest of the cities are truly many cities notwithstanding that their dwellings are in one place, for their politics is for the sake of the governance of the household rather than the governance of the household being for the sake of the governance of the city. Hence if you assemble a single city, that is [only] by accident. The case of the virtuous city and its parts is like the case of the body as a whole: for the hand or the foot,

5 for example, exists only for the body as a whole, [not the body] ⌐for the sake of⌐ its limbs. But the opposite is the case with these cities: their assembling together as a whole is only through a kind of compulsion in order to preserve the household. This is self-evident to one who has even a bit of

44.19   A reference to the conquest of Persia (636-42) by Muslim and non-Muslim Arabs under the command of the Caliph ʿŪmar.

45.1-3   Avempace, *Governance*, 6.2-6, 7.7-11 (*MPP*, pp. 124 f.).

training in this science. In general, as Plato says, these ⌐
cities ⌐first⌐ break down into two cities, one the city of
10 poverty, the other the city of wealth. Furthermore, from
each of these two cities many others branch off. If, in
addition, the impoverished members of this city are given
the possessions of the wealthy, why then waging war against
one of these ignorant cities would be like waging war against
two cities. Hence, this city that we are involved in bringing
forth is in itself great in size and possessed of great power
notwithstanding that it has, as Plato says, but one thousand
15 warriors. For they are like those warriors of whom it is said
that ⌐twenty⌐ free men will vanquish two hundred. Now
since this city will not be of any chance size, the virtuous
community will result from it. It ought not, however, to be
so small that neighboring nations vanquish it, nor so large
that the benefits from plowing, sowing, and the rest would
become costly for them.

20 He said that the rulers ought to determine for them the
extent of this city as to largeness or smallness, and determine
for them, for example, the number of guardians among
them and the proportion of each and every class of artisans. ∟
The case of this city is like the case with natural beings.
Human actions cannot be completed if they are performed
in any happenstance scale of smallness (as is said in tales of
people whose height is a handspan or a cubit), or in any
25 happenstance scale of largeness either (as it is said that in
the past there have been people whose height was sixty
cubits, and the like). Rather [one must take one's bearings
by] the scale that is found in the majority of people. This is

45.11   ignorant cities] Averroes' characterization, taken over from
Farabi and repeated in 52.13-14, 22. See *Political Regime*, 87.5, 87.18-
102.13 (*MPP*, pp. 41, 42-53); and *Virtuous City*, 67.1-69.4 (Dieterici tr.,
pp. 106-109).

45.15-19   This goes beyond Plato 423a, as does the subsequent
discussion.

to be found not only in natural matters but also in artificial
matters, for it is not by any chance measure that there
results from a rhythm the mode for which it was designed.
This being so, a questioner might ask, saying: What will be
46. the extent of this city, and what | will be the number of
guardians in it? We say that this will vary according to the
time, the place, and the nations that are near it. Hence the
actualization of this and [maintaining] its health turn on
the political cogitative faculty—i.e., the experiential faculty
that gauges ⌜these⌝ general things so that they come to
5 exist in matter in actuality. Plato asserts that it suffices if
the guardians in that city—it would seem that this is in
accord with his time and according to the nations that were
near to them—come to one thousand warriors. Galen took
exception to him on this, saying that if he [sc., Plato] had
comprehended ⌜this⌝ time of ours he would know that this
is absurd, alluding thereby to the strength of the realm that
existed in his time. But what appears from Plato is that he
did not make that statement wishing it to be unalterable
10 like the other general things that he mentions here. Rather
he said this in accord with his time and in accord with his
people, i.e., the Greeks. If we see that this city is [not] fit to
wage war with ⌜all⌝ the inhabitants of the earth, could
Plato then not see it? But perhaps someone will say that
Plato meant ⌜only⌝ that no assemblage in a single city ought
to be more than this assemblage—i.e., in a single place.
Moreover, many cities could be taken out of this [one city]
15 in accord with the proper size. Nevertheless, the case of this
gauging [of proper size] also will vary according to the
localities. But each and every one of the virtuous communities ought to be of a limited area, i.e., for each one of

46.1-4 See note to 25.2-8, above.
46.6-8 Presumably this criticism was made in Galen's paraphrase
of the *Republic,* which has not come down to us.

them. Yet if these communities be of a determined number
intended to limit them, then the truth of this ought to be
shown by the conformity of this opinion to the natural
climates or all the natural people. This is alluded to in the
20 saying of the Lawgiver: "I have been sent to the Red and
the Black." If this be the [correct] opinion, Plato does not
favor it; but it is Aristotle's opinion, and it is the indubitable
truth. He says that the lording-it-over expressed by a com- ⌐
mand such as this—i.e., that this city have a limited size—is 423c–
more trifling for them than what we previously ordered   423e
them to do. Namely that it was proper that a bronze son
born to guardians be thrust out among the others [like him],
25 and that a golden or silver son born to these others be thrust
out among the guardians. This is commanded of the
citizens' offspring so that they might be one in nature, since
every one of the humans in it [sc., the city] corresponds to
one particular job, and that is the job for which he is

46.17-19   In opposition to the view just presented of having a large
number of virtuous communities of limited area, Averroes here suggests
the possibility (and immediately hereafter the desirability) of having
a limited number of virtuous communities, each of which might be co-
terminous with an entire climatic zone, perhaps even encompassing all
of mankind. On the causes of the natural differences between nations,
resulting in distinct national characters, see Farabi, *Political Regime*,
70.8-71.9 (*MPP*, pp. 32 f.).

46.19-20   This Tradition (*ḥadīth*) is used elsewhere by Averroes to
point to the universal significance of Muhammad's mission (*Decisive
Treatise*, 7.3-4, 17.9-11 [*MPP*, pp. 169, 178]; *Exposition*, 102.20 [Mueller
tr., p. 95]). Our text here reads *baʿal ha-tōrah*, rather than *maniaḥ ha-tōrah*,
which is also translated later as Lawgiver.

46.20-21   See Józef Bielawski (ed. and trans.), *Lettre d'Aristote à
Alexandre sur la Politique envers les Cités*, Polskiej Akademii Nauk, Komitet
Nauk o Kulturze Antycznej, Archiwum Filologiczne, no. 25 (Wroclaw,
1970), 4.2, 4.5, 10.5 (Arabic text, pp. 33 f., 44; French tr., pp. 59, 60,
66). Compare Aristotle *Politics* 7. 4. 1326a5–b25. For the political
necessity that might require the military conquest of one virtuous city
by another, leading ultimately to the universal sway of a single law, see
Avicenna, *Metaphysics*, 10. 5 (453.10-454.2) (*MPP*, pp. 108 f.).

naturally suited. In general, all these commands and the lording-it-over them to observe all these nomoi and the others that we shall mention hereafter regarding copulation, procreation, and the rest, are no great matter that would
30 afflict people like these. They are all trifling matters for them if they guard them by bringing them up well in the education that we have mentioned—i.e., music and gym-
47. nastic. | Hence one ought to be extremely wary of making ⊢
any innovation in music apart from what the ancient nomoi   424
have laid down. For if this were done, disease would easily be transmitted to the city without anyone's being aware of it. This would not cease by settling calmly and quietly in the dispositions of the soul, but [rather continue] until the matter finally turns into the destruction of the Laws and
5 the nomoi. This is evident from the case of those people who, ⊢
having grown up with such general nomoi and general   425
Laws, are able, by themselves, to arrive at many ⌜partial⌝ nomoi ⌜and good disciplines, such as honoring parents, remaining silent before elders, and other such⌝ practical ⌜nomoi⌝. Hence partial things like these ought not to be laid down as nomoi. That is because the general Laws, when firmly established, will lead the citizens to these partial
10 nomoi easily and by themselves because everyone only moves toward that which his upbringing in discipline and ⌜his⌝ nature move him toward. If [they are] good, then [it is toward the] good, or if [they are] bad, then [it is toward the] bad. But if one strives to lay down these partial nomoi without laying down the general ones (as happens to many ⌜legislators⌝), why he is on the level of one who would ⊢
heal diseased people who are unable to derive any benefit   426
from that by which they might be healed on account of their excessive desire for food, drink, and copulation. That
15 is because their diseases will change markedly for the worse on account of these medicines. Hence anyone who strives to

lay down partial nomoi such as these will not cease improving their affairs ⌐as long as he lives⌐, and they will rely
on him. He will think that he is attaining an end thereby,
but he will not attain it. You can make this clear from the
cases of many of the legislators whose accounts have reached
us. The case of striving to improve these cities is, as Plato
20 says, like one cutting off a single head of the [many-]headed
serpents. He is doing something useless since they will emit
their poison with their remaining heads. This being so, one
ought at first only to lay down general nomoi like these,
which have already been mentioned and which will be
spoken of yet again in this book. He said: But as for the
nomos to be laid down concerning temples, prayers, sacri-
25 fices, and offerings, which will imprint in the souls humility
and the extolling of God and the angels, why he would
leave them to what God (may He be exalted!) commands
through prophecy. It is as though he asserts that these are
divine things, and that whatever of these there is in ⌐cities⌐
we ought to acknowledge as such, for they [sc., the divine
things] are, as it were, common to all the Laws and conventions of the nomoi. Since Plato, at the beginning of this
book, had already investigated what justice is and refuted
30 what was said concerning justice by the opinions generally
accepted in ⌐his⌐ time, he promised first to make known
48. the nature of | justice in the city and then to make known
the nature of justice in the individual soul, being as it is
more evident in a city. He said: An example of this would
be if a particular man were ordered to read a script with

(margin: 427a–427c)

(margin: 368de)

47.24-26   In addition to substituting prophecy for the Delphic Apollo
of Plato 427b, Averroes supplies on his own the reasons for this nomos.
Humility does not appear in the *Republic*.

47.26-28   Knowledge of these divine things comes through prophecy
since these transcend ordinary human understanding. Though superhuman in this sense, these things are not peculiar to the Koran, but are
to be found in every *sharī'a* and in every nomos.

tiny letters from afar, and we knew that the selfsame book
5 with large letters was to be found in another place close by
him. We comprehend that it is right that we direct [our
attention] first to that book with broad lines and read it
first. And after we comprehend it, then it will be possible
for us to read the book with tiny letters with ease. Similar
to this is the ⌜case⌝ with justice in the city and in the
particular soul. But as we have said, before making known
the nature of justice through definition, he began to explain
how life in the just city is. Having reached this point in it
[sc., the *Republic*], he wished to make known the nature of
10 justice since it could already be seen quite clearly there
from what he says about the life of the city. Similarly, it is ⊢—
also evident from this very thing [sc., from the life of the   427e–
city] that it [sc., the city] is wise, courageous, moderate,   428
⌜and just. He proceeded⌝ to investigate what is the nature
of each one of these four virtues that exist in this city, and
in which part of it it is to be found. He began with wisdom,
saying that it is clear that this city is wise, possessing
15 knowledge. That is because it [displays] fine understanding
in all things to which the Laws and nomoi point, which we
ourselves will mention by recounting them. Good governance and good counsel are undoubtedly a kind of knowledge. But ⌜we⌝ cannot say that good governance and good
counsel are in this city on account of wisdom in the practical
arts such as agriculture, carpentry, and so on. Since this is
so, then it [sc., the city] can ⌜only⌝ be wise through that
20 knowledge on whose track we are. It is evident that this
wisdom can only be completed through knowledge of the
end of man since this governance moves in that direction.
And it is evident that we can only perceive the end of man

48.19-23 Farabi, *Attainment*, 15.16-16.5, 16.15-17.9, 20.3-22.5,
26.11-19, 39.9-40.2 (*MPP*, pp. 61 f., 64 f., 67 f., 76 f.); *Political Regime*,
79.3-80.4 (*MPP*, pp. 36 f.).

through the theoretical sciences. Hence this city is necessarily spoken of as wise in two kinds of knowledge simul-
taneously—i.e., the theoretical and the practical. That part
in which this wisdom will be is the smallest of its [sc., the
25 city's] parts, namely the philosophers. That is because these
natures occur less frequently than the other natures—i.e.,
[the natures of] the possessors of practical arts. It is evident
that this wisdom ought to be firmly established in the ruler
of the city and rule over it. This being so, the heads of this
city are necessarily the wise. We have then told of the
knowledge on whose account this city is said to be wise and
in which of its parts [it resides]. | ⊢

49.   As for the courage ascribed to this city, why it consists in   429–
preserving this opinion as explained and seeking to strength-   430b
en it in all natural people in every case of strength and
weakness. By "strength" I mean such as fear and anxiety;
by "weakness," such as the desires. It is evident that the
multitude in this part will be of ⌜this⌝ character only if we
inculcate in them the characteristics that we have men-
5 tioned and try them by means of ⌜those⌝ proofs—i.e., music
and gymnastic. For once they are of this character it will
be difficult for fear or desire to uproot this opinion from
their ⌜souls⌝. But if, in the course of their being governed,
they imagine these things [sc., fear and desire], it would be
easy to remove and transfer this opinion from their souls.

48.25   the philosophers] Averroes' substitution for Plato 428e: the
supervising and ruling part.
49.1-5   According to Plato 429b, a city is called courageous by virtue
of the courage of that part which does its fighting for it. Similarly
Averroes in this text (24.7-8, 49.16-21). Yet here a "multitude" is seen
as being, in some sense, courageous; and all "natural people" are to
receive some kind of education in music and gymnastic. Such termi-
nology underlines, as it were, the qualified character of this courage,
expressed by its designation as "political courage" in Plato 430c. True,
unqualified courage goes beyond the city and, as such, is not to be
expected from all "natural people."

An image of this is, as Plato says, what dyers do. When they
want to dye camlet so that it is colorfast, they first ⌜choose⌝
white from among the colors of the garment. Then they
10 prepare it beforehand and ready it with not a few things to
receive the color so that the camlet receives the color in as
good a manner as possible; so that when the color is put
down and permeates it, it is impossible to eradicate it by
washing it with scouring agents. As for the garment that
has not been so prepared, its color will be washed out from
it when washed with scouring agents. So is the case with
the guardians. If they are not brought up with the education
15 we have described and if their natures are not chosen [with
deliberation], it is doubtful whether this opinion will [not]
be eradicated from their souls and its color removed, for
pleasure is the most powerful scourer of the virtues and
most effective in eradicating them. Similarly with anxiety
and fear.   ⊢—

It is clear in what thing of this city this virtue—i.e.,   429b
courage—is to be found and also to which part it is to be
ascribed. This can ⌜only⌝ be ascribed to it [by virtue of]
these people whose natures we have chosen for guardianship
and whom we have arranged to maintain this part. For it
20 is clear that cities are not said to be courageous or timid in
all their parts or in just any part—i.e., the moneyed class
or the ⌜class⌝ [engaged in] the practical arts—but only in
the guardian class.   L

We have then perceived what this virtue is and to which
of the parts of the city it is to be ascribed. It remains for us ⌜
to speak of the two remaining virtues, namely moderation   430de
and justice: what they are, and to which of the parts of the
city they are to be ascribed.
25 We say that moderation is some middle way in eating,
drinking, and copulation. The moderate one is the individual who, on his own, can always be on this middle way.

That is why it is said that moderation is some kind of
conquest and forcing of the soul from pleasures and desires.
It has been said that the moderate one is more powerful
and stronger than himself. This means that, seeing that man ⊢
has in him a nobler part—namely reason—and a base   431
part—namely the appetitive soul—if the nobler is more
30 powerful and stronger than the baser and the baser is in
submission to it, then it is said that this man is stronger
than himself. But if he is humbled by the baser, whether
because of upbringing or otherwise, it is said that he is
50. weaker than himself and licentious. | This being so, it is
evident that this city will be more powerful than the others
and stronger than ⌐itself⌐ and that this virtue ought not to
be in one particular class of citizens ⌐but in the rulers⌐ and
the general multitude. For not a single human activity is
called human for the virtue that it attains other than
moderation. The case here is not like the case with wisdom
5 and courage, which are ascribed to the city in that they
are in a part of it. This virtue, however, ought to be spread ⊢
throughout the city ⌐and⌐ transmitted to the generality   432ab
from the beginning of [its] growth in one way—i.e., the
unanimity in it. Its opposite should be rejected. We have
said, then, what moderation is and how it is ascribed to the
city. The fourth virtue remains, the investigation of which
10 goes back to the beginning of the matter, namely justice.

We say that equity in this city—and self-control, which ⊢
is the work of justice—is nothing more than what we were   433a–
saying it was in the previous account concerning the govern-   433d
ance of this city. ⌐Namely, we ourselves have already said

49.30   man] MSS: part.
49.32   weaker than himself and licentious] Following Plato 431b.
More literally, but less intelligibly: that he is more fully submissive in
his soul and that he is irreversible.
50.6   unanimity] Following Plato 432a; MSS: the quickness.

that every single one of the people in this city ought to lay
hold⌐ onto [only] one ⌐of the activities of the city⌐: namely
that activity to which he is disposed by nature. ⌐This is
that⌐ equity which gives preservation and duration to the
15 city as long as it is to be found persisting in it, and it gives it
the three powers that we have finished discussing. This will
be when the opinion of the lords and the multitude concur
in ⌐preserving⌐ what the nomoi oblige them to, so that this
disposition comes to be found in the youth, women, slaves,
freeborn, rulers, and multitude, and in general in all its
parts. That is, every one of them will perform the activity
that is his by nature and will not long for what does not
20 belong to him. This being so, this city will be just in ⌐their
associating together in it⌐, for the equity in it consists ⌐only⌐
in every one of its citizens doing what is singularly his.
This is political justice; just as perversion in cities, which is ⊢—
the cause of injustice, is nothing more than each and every   434
one of its citizens growing up in more than one thing and
transfering ⌐from thing⌐ to thing, from activity to activity,
and from rank to rank—and this, notwithstanding that it is
25 thought not to be harmful to the city in the practical arts.
Its harm will be very evident in the transfer of classes from
one to the other, as when one who is parsimonious and
wealthy is transferred, [thanks] to his parsimony, so as to
enter the class of warriors or, even more, the class of chiefs.
51. This leads to many evils. You can make this clear | from
[what happens in these] cities. It has then been made clear
from this statement what justice is and that it is something
that exists spread over all parts of this city.

50.15   the three powers] I.e., the three virtues.
50.21   Aristotle *Nicomachean Ethics* 5. 6-7. 1134a25-1135a14. The
term "political justice" does not appear in the *Republic*.
50.26, 27   class] Plato's *eidos*. Rather than the usual *sūg*, *hakhanah*
is used here.

When he had finished making known the nature of justice in cities, he set out to consider whether it is the selfsame thing in the individual soul. If this in fact corresponds to what was said of this in the city, then it is right. If not, then he would reconsider what was said of this in the city. For things differing [only] in smallness and greatness are of one class, and there is nothing in the one that is contrary to what is in the other. Hence whatever must necessarily be justice and equity in the individual soul is the selfsame thing in ⌜the⌝ individual city.

He said: We have already said that equity in the city consists in each of the three natures—i.e., the calculating nature, the spirited nature, and the appetitive nature—doing what is appropriate for it in the appropriate measure and in the ⌜appropriate⌝ time.⌜ It is on account of this⌝ that we say of this city that it is wise, courageous, and moderate. ⌜Even if⌝ these three kinds exist in the individual soul, there is neither self-control nor justice in the individual soul unless these faculties exist in the true manner in which they exist in the city, so that the cogitative part rules over the other faculties and the other faculties are in submission to it. It is clear from this that if these faculties were not in the soul it would be impossible for them to be in the city, for these things cannot exist in it other than through humans. It has already been made clear in physics that there are two opposing faculties in us: one, cogitation; the other, appetite. This is evident in that we may have an appetite for some-

⌐ 435

⌐ 439d–442a

51.10 *tebha' ha-habhanah*—calculating, in the sense of reasoning, deducing.

51.13 The faculties of the soul must be in the same relation to each other as are their analogues in the virtuous city.

51.17-18 cogitation . . . appetite] Plato 439d speaks of *logismos* and *alogiston*. Aristotle *De Anima* 3. 9. 432a26 refers to *logon* and *alogon*. (Cf. *Nicomachean Ethics* I. 13. 1102a26-28: this is an exoteric distinction.) See also *De Anima* 3. 10. 433a9 ff.

thing and yet not do it. Appetite is partly desire and partly
20 spiritedness. It is also evident in that spiritedness oftens wars
against desire and rules over it as though it were an instrument of ascendancy ⌐by⌐ which it [sc., cogitation] rules over
them. Hence it is that we frequently grow angry at what
the desires bring [us] to thoughtlessly. If all this is as we
have characterized it, these three faculties exist in the soul
in the way they do in the individual city. Indeed, the cause
of their being in the city is the very cause of their being in
25 the individual soul. The justice and equity in the individual
soul consist in every one of its parts doing what it has to do,
as is the case in the city. Hence the cogitative kind will be
ruling if it is wise or helped by the entire soul. And the
spirited kind will obey and submit to it, heatedly aroused
by it ⌐and⌐ battling with the other kind [sc., the desiring
kind]. This harmony in the individual soul is achieved
52.   through music and gymnastic. For gymnastic | strengthens
the spirited soul and gives it courage, while music renders it
disciplined, submissive to cogitation. If these two parts grow
up in accord with this description, they will turn to that
other part and discipline it. The particular individual is
called wise precisely on account of that part because of
5 which we called the city wise; and the names "courageous"
and "moderate" are predicated of the very same parts. For ⊢—
the courageous individual is one who always preserves what   **442cd**
cogitation orders and commands him—by "always" I mean
through times of fears and anxieties and desires. ⌐Thus⌐, in
what has preceded, we have been defining political courage.
Similarly, the wise individual is only he in whom the
cogitative part forever rules over the other parts, ⌐as⌐ is the
case ⌐in⌐ the city. Similarly, the case of the moderation of
10 the ⌐particular⌐ individual is the same as the case of the

51.21   thoughtlessly] Literally: without cogitation.

moderation of the city. Hence, the individual stamped with the nature of this city will be of the utmost virtue just as this city is of the utmost virtue.

It has then been made clear from this that the equity and justice in the individual soul are identical with the equity and justice in the city. From this it can be seen that the ⊢— deceit and injustice in the individual soul are identical with 444 the deceit and injustice in the ignorant cities. This is nothing more than when one of these ⌜faculties⌝ that is not fit to rule
15 sets itself up as chief and rules over them, as when the spirited soul or ⌜the desiring soul⌝ rules. The case here is like the case with the body's health and disease. Just as its health consists only in the equibalance of the humors and nature's ruling over it, and its disease consists ⌜only⌝ in their being dispersed contrary to nature and their ruling over it, so is the case with the soul. Its health consists in its linking up with the cogitative part, and its disease consists in its [sc., some other part of the soul's] ruling over it [sc., the cogitative part]. Thus virtue is some kind of health and beauty, and vice is some kind of disease. Just as health is ⊢—
20 one, so is virtue one. Hence the virtuous city is one. The 445cd vices, however, are many and varied, just as the diseases are many and varied. Hence the ignorant cities are many and varied, save that they are comprehended under four classes, according to what he says later on. The virtuous governance has two designations: One is kingship, ⌜and
25 that is when [there is only] one who is in charge of it. The second is aristocracy⌝, and that is when ⌜they have⌝ more

---

52.13-14   ignorant cities] Plato 444a–b speaks of lack of learning. See note to 45.11, above.

52.25-26   aristocracy] Consider Averroes' comments in his epitome of Aristotle's *Metaphysics*, *Kitāb ʿilm mā baʿd al-ṭabīʿa*: "In general, the case with the world is like the case with the city of good [men] [or: the aristocratic city]. For even though it has many rulers, it ascends to a single rulership and aims at a single end; otherwise it would not be one

chiefs than one. Having completed the statement con- ⌐
cerning the classes of virtues that are in this city, he returns
to what remains in the case of the guardians, namely the
inquiry concerning how they copulate, the upbringing of
their children, and the manner of their procreation.

We say that it is clear that if we wish the natures of these
30 guardians to be preserved through procreation—i.e., that
for the most part they should procreate their like—it cannot
be that they copulate with any chance women, | but [rather
53. only with] women who resemble them in nature ⌐and who⌐
have grown up with something like that training. This is
obligatory not only for guardians but for each and every
class of citizens. Hence it is [a subject] fit for investigation
whether there exist among women natures resembling the
natures of each and every class of citizens—and in particular
the guardians—or whether women's natures are distinguished from men's natures. If the former is the case, then
5 as regards the activities of the city, women would have the
very same standing as men in those classes, so that there
would be among them warriors, philosophers, rulers, and
the rest. But if this is not the case, then women are only fit
in the city for activities that men in general are unfit for,
as if you were to say upbringing, procreation, and the like.

And we say that women, in so far as they are of one kind
10 with men, necessarily share in the end of man. They will
differ only in less or more; i.e., the man in most human
activities is more diligent than the women, though it is not
impossible that women should be more diligent in some

[city]. But just as it is in this way that the city continues to exist, so is
the case with the world. Hence the household cities (*al-mudun al-
manziliyya*) decay quickly, for the unity that they possess is in a way only
accidental" (*Compendio de Metafísica*, ed. and Spanish trans. by Carlos
Quirós Rodríguez [Madrid: Maestre, 1919], 4.39 [Arabic text, p. 145];
German trans. by S. Van den Bergh, *Die Epitome der Metaphysik des
Averroes* [Leiden: Brill, 1924], p. 123). See note to 79.1-8, below.

activities, such as is thought concerning the art of practical
music. That is why it is said of melodies that they are
perfected when men produce them and women do them
15 well. If this is so, and the nature of men and women is of one
kind, and the ⌐nature⌐ that is of one kind ⌐turns⌐ to only
one activity in the city, then it is evident that the women in
this city will practice the [same] activities as the men,
except that they are weaker at it. Hence it is obligatory
that the less recondite activities be handed over to them.
This will be brought to light with evident clarity through
20 investigation. We see women sharing arts with men except
that they are weaker at it, although most of the women in
[some] art may be more diligent than the men, as in the art
of weaving, sewing, and other such ⌐arts. As for⌐ their
sharing in the art of war and the rest, why this is made clear
from the inhabitants of deserts and the "City of Women"
[Dāghūda]. Similarly, too, since some women are formed
25 with eminence and a praiseworthy disposition, it is not
impossible that there be philosophers and rulers among
them. Since it was thought that this class existed only
infrequently among them, some Laws ruled out women's
being priests—i.e., the high priesthood. Some [other] Laws,
however, not ruling out [the possibility] of this existing
among them, rejected ⌐this⌐. This is already clear from
investigation of the animals—i.e., that it is fitting that there

53.23   This is the famous "City of Women" whose inhabitants were
every bit as tough as the Jalāliqah (see note to 27.9, above). Idrīsī,
Nuzhah, MS Bibliothèque Nationale (Paris), No. 2221, fol. 344a, says
that it is an island in the Atlantic and can be reached from the city of
Dāghūda (among others), of which the Daghūr (or Dajūr!) of MS *A*
may be a variant. El-Hajji, in his edition of al-Bakrī, *Geography*, pp.
169-170, gives other references for the City of Women (Mahdi).
Rosenthal, accepting emendations of Baneth and Levi della Vida, translates "inhabitants of deserts and frontier villages." See Rosenthal, 1966
reprinting, p. 165, n. 3.

53.24   eminence] or: clarity, purity. *zkhūth* or *zakūth*.

be female guardians. This refers to the animals to whom we
54. previously compared the guardian. We see this | in female
dogs who guard what their males guard and strike at hyenas
just as their males strike at them, save that they are weaker
at this. That is why nature sometimes, but rarely, gives the
male an instrument with which he can fight that is not in
the female, ⌐as is the case with the boar⌐. But since the
fighting instruments of those animals whose wont it is to
fight are for the most part common to the male and the
female, it [sc., nature] intends that the female also perform
5 this activity. The competence of women is unknown, however, in these cities since they are only taken ⌐in them⌐ for
procreation and hence are placed at the service of their
husbands and confined to procreation, upbringing, and
suckling. This nullifies their [other] activities. Since women
in these cities are not prepared with respect to any of the
human virtues, they frequently resemble plants in these
10 cities. Their being a burden upon the men ⌐in these cities⌐
is one of the causes of the poverty of these cities. This is
because they are to be found there in double the number of
men, while not understanding through [their] upbringing
any of the necessary actions except for the few actions—like
the art of spinning and weaving—that they undertake
mostly at a time when they have need of them to make up
for their lack of spending [power]. This is all self-evident.
This being so—and it is clear from the case of the females
15 that they are to share with the males in war and the rest—it
is fitting that, in choosing them, we seek for those very
natures that we sought for in the men and that they should
be trained in the same way through music and gymnastic.

He said: They have no ⌐cover⌐ on them when they ⌐
practice gymnastic with the men, since they will be devoid 457a

----

54.11 necessary] I.e., in contradistinction to noble activities.

of [everything save] virtue. When it became clear to ⌐him¬
that the women will stand guard ⌐just as¬ the man does,
and that these female guardians will be with the men in
the same place—since none of those who are virtuous
20 guardians in this city has a dwelling ⌐in which¬ to isolate ⊢
himself—and that their meals are to be taken as one, he   458c-
                                                            458e
said that necessity undoubtedly will bring them [sc., the
women] to desire copulation. But copulation ought not to
be permitted them whenever they wish and with whomever
they wish, since we wish that this activity be human among
them and that their copulations not be of any chance
character. The arrangement of their procreation will be the
best possible with respect to their conditions of guardianship, but at fixed times and with determined individuals
25 and characteristics. This is, as it were, common to the other ⌊
conventions and Laws, though as it appears the adherents
of the Laws differ from one another in the force of the
statements. We ourselves will explain here briefly what
Plato asserts about these things.

We say: As for the time during which these guardians ⌐
will engage in copulation, he holds that its determination   459-
                                                             460
turns on the preservation of their kind. Thus also the
increase or diminution [in frequency] of copulation: this
55.   varies in accord with the wars that occur | and other such
things that necessitate an increase in copulation or its
diminution. As for which individual in this city should
copulate with which other individual, why [they should be]
the ⌐individuals¬ who resemble one another ⌐with a view¬
to preserving the good natures in their offspring. When one

54.21   he said] A new paragraph begins here in MS *A*.

54.21   to desire copulation] Plato 458d does not single out women in
this respect.

54.23   human] Plato 458d: holy.

54.26   adherents of the Laws] or: religionists.

55.1, 2   individual(s)] *praṭ*, rather than the usual *īsh*, is used here.

wishes to raise hunting dogs or raptorial birds, he takes care
to mate the excellent natures with the excellent nature so
5 that the offspring will be of that character. All the more
ought care to be taken of this matter in this city. This is
precisely why it ought not to be permitted in the city for
anyone, with a view to having children, to copulate at any
age he wishes, but [only] during the prime years, namely—
as Plato says—from twenty to thirty in women and in men
from thirty to fifty-five. As for the arrangement under which
10 he holds it to be proper for these guardians to copulate and
have children, why it is that these women be common to
all the men, no one woman living alone with one man as is
the case in these cities, and that their children also be
common. As for the community of women, it is to be of
this character: namely that the women dwell together with
all the men, only without copulation being permitted them.
When the rulers hold that necessity points to procreation,
15 they order that weddings for grooms and brides be celebrat-
ed in the city. They bring sacrifices, offer donations, and
institute prayers in which they call on God (may He be
exalted!) that He may be gracious unto them; and they
order that a poem be sung using verses and lines suitable
for weddings. In general they take the meetings of the
citizens [as occasions for] these gatherings. Then, after this,
the men and women gather together; and they [sc., the
rulers], acting subtly in the drawing of lots, draw lots among
them for the women. The drawing of lots makes it appear
20 that whatever befalls each and every woman is only something begotten by chance and accident. Thus [the men]
hold that [the women] are common to them [all], but in

55.4, 7   excellent, prime] The same word as that translated as
"virtuous."

55.8   Plato 460e: A woman's prime is from twenty to forty; a man's
from twenty-five to fifty-five.

fact the drawing of lots concerns what is to be born among comparable kinds. That is, the good kind of women are allotted to the good kind of men, and the bad to the bad, without any of the citizens other than the lords being aware of this. (Galen has mentioned that there is a book ⌜of his⌝ on this kind of drawing of lots; it is the one called *Deceptive*

25 *Lottery*.) By proceeding in this way two [advantageous] things are joined: first, what they hold concerning the community of women; second, the preservation of the good nature in procreation. What can be imagined with regard to one of these [classes] can be imagined as well in many [other] respects. |

56.   He said: Then the women ⌜are separated⌝ from the men and dwell with those among them who are pregnant until their delivery. When they have been delivered of children, it is incumbent upon them not to see their children; the 460cd offspring are transferred to one another or to governesses and wet-nurses if the mothers do not have enough for suckling. This ⌜he did⌝ in order that they see that they have their children in common so that every one of them 461c- 461e

5 holds the offspring of all members of ⌜that⌝ class to be his children, and the children hold all these parents to be their parents. And all this is for the sake of love. This being so, there are no relatives in this city other than parents, grand-parents, sons, daughters, grandchildren, brothers, and sisters. This city has ranks: child is an acknowledged rank, and parent is an acknowledged rank, and similarly the

10 rank of grandparents; so that all children wax in praise of all the parents in the manner in which parents [customarily] are esteemed, and the parents love all the children with the love with which children [customarily] are loved. That

55.24   *Deceptive Lottery*] According to Baneth, the Hebrew corresponds to *qurʿat idhān*.

56.9   child . . . and parent] or: son . . . and father.

is why the copulations in this city are only between brothers
and sisters. ⌜But the copulation of parents with children is
forbidden since they [sc., the children] are lower [in rank];
similarly that of children with parents since they [sc., the
parents] are higher [in rank]⌝. And this is so ⌜only⌝ so that   ⌞
parental esteem not be mixed with the contempt associated
15 with copulation, nor filial love with the love of [sexual]
desire. Once ⌜the children's⌝ esteem for parents fails, the
city necessarily is ruined. This cause is operative in all
Laws, even though they differ from one another in deter-
mining this [and even though] their nomoi too are not
congruent with one another. Age is one of the conditions
laid down concerning copulation. As to whether one who
has passed the years for copulation [i.e., the prescribed
years for procreation] is permitted to copulate in the city
for the sake of ejecting the superfluous [semen in his body]—
20 since of the superfluities the ejection of this is most truly
necessary—why there is room for inquiry here. Plato permits   ⌜
it on condition that no offspring of theirs be seen [alive] in   461c
the city. But this [copulation] too ought to be determined   ⌞
according to what will preserve health. It is evident that
these weddings are to be repeated among them according
to the need for procreation—i.e., frequently or seldom—
since this city indeed is to be of a fixed size forever. This
also depends on how many women become pregnant at
each and every wedding. Galen, due to his ignorance of
Plato's intention, became confused in trying to understand
25 from Plato whether or not these weddings ought to be
repeated. For if they are not repeated, each and every man
is left with a particular woman; and therewith the community [of women] ceases and mutual love is negated. Each
one of them will love to bring good things for his or her
spouse more than he will love doing so for others; and it
will turn into [a city of] households, not a single city. This

57.   is clear to one who has been trained in this | science. This
being so, it is even more farfetched than all this to permit
an individual to dwell in a separate house, for no one in
this city possesses any thing of his own. Rather, the case of
their community is like the case of the community of the
limbs of the body. A man ought only to copulate with
women during those weddings for that measure of time
that he knows the woman is most likely to become impreg-
nated. This, then, is what Plato asserts concerning the
community of children and women.

5   Then, after this, he undertakes to bring proof of the
necessity of these communities. He begins, saying: He who ⌐
governs these cities is obliged in his governance to aim for ⁴⁶²
the greatest good for the city just as he ought to remove the
greatest evil from them. Now there is no greater evil in the
governance of the city than that governance which converts
a single city into many cities, just as there is no greater good
in cities than that which joins them together and makes
10   them one. This being so, it is clear that community in
advantages and damages will lead them to be bound to
the city and befriend it. This is because the citizens, if they
live, all live together, and if they are killed, are killed
together. Their joys and their sorrows in this are of a piece.
The separation of the citizens and the removal of each from
his fellow in such matters as these confuses them and
destroys their assemblage. This is when some of them are
15   joyful and others of them sorrowful, even sometimes [going
to the point] that some of them rejoice in the sorrow of
others. That is why it is said that people's being near other
people is advantageous. In general, there is nothing more
productive of evil and confusion to the city than its citizens'
saying of some particular thing, "This is mine and this is
not mine." As for the cities in which what is laid down for
one is laid down for the association [as a whole] and what

befalls him is closer to being what befalls all, why that is the
20 city that is joined, compounded together, and natural. For
the case of the community between the parts of these cities
and the cities is like the case of the community between the
limbs of an animal's body and the rest of the body as regards
pain and pleasure. The entire body is pained by a single
finger's hurt so that this pain is confirmed upon the whole
body and one says that it is feeling weak. The same is the
case with joys and pleasures. All this being as we have └
characterized it and since the cities whose association we
wish to be virtuous ought to be of this kind, why it is evident
25 that that community of children and women of which we
have spoken is one of the most necessary of things. For it ┌
will not be possible for any one of these guardians to 463cd
designate another as either unrelated to him or as a relative.
Rather, every one of them whom he encounters he will hold
to be his father or grandfather or mother or grandmother
or brother or sister or son or daughter. Hence, as we have
said, they will treat parents with shame before them and
30 esteem of them as prescribed by the general nomos. This is ⊢
58.   the greatest good for the city—i.e., that in joys | and 464
damages its parts be to its whole as the case of the limbs of
a single body to the body. The case of the community of
children and women resembles their community of property. That is why we said that it is not fitting that any one of
them have a dwelling of his own or something by which he
would be isolated so that one of them would dwell in his
house without ⌜the others⌝ as much as it was possible for
5 him to do so, and the others also would do likewise. Still
less ought he to have a child of his own and women of his
own [for thereby] evils of his own and damages of his own
will come to pass, sometimes ⌜being⌝—as we have said—a

58.8   women] Plato 464e: relatives.

cause of the growth of evils besetting others. This is the cause of the disputes occurring among citizens of this city over money, children, and women. It is evident that if all the things in this city are in accord with this, then it will
10 remove envy and hatred from them as well as poverty and the other evils found in these cities. Hence there will be no need in them [sc., the citizens of this city] for instituting fines on account of the taking of property, theft, and other such things as occur in these cities. Rather, these people are of the utmost elevation and happiness. They are indeed happy. They are beset by none of the evils besetting the citizens of these cities. All of this is self-evident to one who has investigated these associations.

15 After it became clear to him that these communities [of children, women, and property] were necessary and that the women ought to guard along with the men—i.e., the women of the guardians—whether standing guard in the city or going out to war, just as female dogs do with their males—i.e., that they share with them in everything having to do with guardianship—he undertook to investigate whether their children [too] ought to go out to war for the sake of becoming expert in it by observing them, as is done in the other arts, so that when they had become perfected
20 they would begin doing it. This happens in many of the arts, such as the art of smiths and others, who keep their children in their presence so that they might for a time observe them and what comes out of it [sc., the art]. This is prior to their doing anything [themselves], for there is no ⌜small⌝ difference between learners who contemplate the crafts from the very outset and those who do not observe. Since this exists in the other arts, all the more should this be
25 the case with the guardians' children, considering that we wish guardians of the utmost expertness to emerge from them. Moreover, when their children go out to war their

466c–
466e

467

zeal for killing is strengthened, as one sees happening with
most animals. When fighting in the presence of its offspring,
it becomes more emboldened thereby than by all other
things. However, it is not intended that the youths, on
account of their softness and weakness, should be killed
while attending the parents or that they should on occasion
endanger ⌜their [parents'] lives⌝. Hence their parents, who
59.   possess the requisite knowledge, ⌜ought⌝ to consider | [the
chances of] war. Whoever among them [sc., the youth] is
timid will not go forth to it, and whoever of them is without
timidity will go forth to it. Also, this is to occur [only]
⌜after⌝ they have become proficient at riding horses. We
shall cunningly provide for their security [by making them
mount] old horses, and they shall be in a place from which
they may view the battle. They shall lay down nomoi in ⊢—
this city that anyone who leaves the center of battle or   468a
5   throws away ⌜his⌝ arms or does any act of cowardice and
weakness shall come back to be one of the artisans who
work with their hands. As for whichever of them is seized
prisoner, we only deliver him to the enemies without our
caring about him evermore since he has so entangled himself on his own that he was caught as a ram is caught. Hence ⊢—
a nomos ought ⌜to be laid down⌝ that they are not to strip   469c–
the dead, for many an army has been lost through this   469e
activity—excepting whichever of them takes his [sc., the
10 slain's] weapons, needing to take weapons only because his
own knife or sword has been broken. And Plato permits ⊢—
every one of these guardians, while in camp, to welcome   468b–
                                                             468e

59.6-10   The reason given for indifference to the fate of soldiers held
prisoner by the enemy is Averroes' own. In leaping over from 468a to
469c–d, Averroes may be suggesting that soldiers are captured and
armies defeated because they are diverted from the fighting by the
prospect of battlefield looting. Such prisoners are not worth a moment's
thought.

whomever he wishes and kiss him for this will lead them to
fight [more eagerly].

He said: It is fitting that the choicest of these guardians
be honored with singular honors in the city, with sacrifices
and offerings being brought to them and eulogies and songs
15 composed about them. ⌜As for⌝ those of them who die in ⊢
war, why it is obligatory to speak of those who die in this 469a–
way as turning into angels walking on earth, pure and holy, 469c
guarding humans against falling into evils and vices. It is
also fitting to ⌜bury⌝ them in [a unique manner and in a
unique place and to use their ⌜tombs⌝ as temples in which
to pray. Something like this is done with one who has died
otherwise than through having been killed [in battle] if he
was praiseworthy in conduct.

20   When he completed this he investigated whether the
citizens ought to enslave one who was of their class and
[spoke] their language in common with them—by "class" ⊢
I mean the stock and the place—or whether the brunt of 470–
war upon them ought to reach [the point of] burning down 471b
their houses and cutting down ⌜their trees⌝. He said that it
was not fitting that this class, which is one, do this to its
own class. Thus, it is not fitting that Greeks, for example,
enslave Greeks, burn down their houses, and cut down their
trees. It is more fitting that what is like this be called
25 severing and mutilation rather than be called war, for such
a war resembles the strife that breaks out between members
60. of a single household or between lovers. | When, therefore,
this strife breaks out among some class of people, the
guardians ought to lay down a nomos for them not to
destroy their houses, cut down their trees, or enslave them. ⌞
These are to be called ones who have gone astray, not

59.16   angels] A near-quotation from Hesiod in Plato 469a is further
altered by Averroes' substituting "angels" for "demons."
59.18   pray] Plato 469a: worship at the tombs as at those of demons.

unbelievers. What Plato asserts differs from what many
Lawgivers assert.

5   He said: As for any not of their class, why it is permissible ⌐
for the guardians to do all these acts to them. This, then, is   471b
the explanation of what Plato says concerning the training ⌊
of this particular class of the city—i.e., the guardians—and
how there is community among them. You ought to know
that much of what he says concerning community and
upbringing in music and gymnastic is common to all classes
of the city, even though gymnastic differs from class to class.
Similarly with the fictions that they transmit to them
10   through music: namely that every kind be moved by the
affective speeches only toward the activity designated for it
by nature. Only Plato does not lay this down so as to
mention these things for each and every class of citizens
since this depends in proximate potentiality on what he
said about the guardians. What we have yet to set apart in
discourse is the speech concerning the class of the wise, as
he did subsequently. We shall speak concerning the recog-

60.4   The command to exterminate idolaters ought to be understood
as an act required by "human opinion," not as an expression of God's
vengefulness, according to Maimonides, *Guide*, I 54 (66a) (Pines tr.,
pp. 126 f.). Consider also Averroes' remarks on extirpative war in his
Middle Commentary on the *Nicomachean Ethics*, 1137b24: "And you can
understand this from the laws laid down with respect to war in the Law
of the Muslims because the command in it pertaining to war is very
general to such a point that they destroy, root and branch, whoever
differs with them. Now there are times in which peace is more to be
preferred than war. However, since the Muslim multitude make this
edict of war generally valid despite the impossibility of destroying their
enemies completely, great damage has attained them on account of
their ignorance of the intention of the Lawgiver, the blessings of God
be upon him. It is therefore proper to say that peace is preferable at
times to war." The Hebrew text and English translation appear in the
review of Rosenthal by Lawrence V. Berman, *Oriens*, 20 (1968-1969):
439. This subject is treated with delicacy in Avicenna, *Metaphysics*, 10. 5
(453.2-454.2) (*MPP*, pp. 108 f.).

60.7-12   See note to 49.1-5, above.

nition of the natures that are disposed to this; and what is
15 the manner of training them; and, when they have become
perfected, what is the manner of their rule and lordship
over the city. We make this the conclusion of the first
treatise of this epitome.

The Second Treatise

Since this governance can only come into being if it is possible—and perchance happens—that the king is a philosopher, and since this also holds for ⌜its⌝ preservation after it has come into being, and since it was his intention
20 to speak of the natures of these [individuals] and the manner of their education, he began first by describing the philosopher. He said: He is the one who longs for knowledge of what is and inquiry into its nature apart from matter. This may be discerned, according to his opinion, in the statement concerning forms. You ought to know that the philosopher, according to the primary intention, is the one who has attained the theoretical sciences [by virtue of] the four conditions that have been enumerated in the book on
25 demonstration. One of those conditions is that he have the ability to discover them [sc., the theoretical sciences] and to teach them. There are two ways of teaching them: One of them is the way of teaching the elect few; this is teaching by demonstrative arguments. The second is the teaching of
61. the multitude; this is teaching | by persuasive and poetical arguments. It is evident that this will not be fulfilled in him unless he is wise in practical science and moreover has the cogitative virtue by which those things that have been explained in practical science are brought about in nations and cities, and has the great moral virtue by which the
5 governance of cities and justice are chosen. Hence, if the

60.26   See 25.14-33, above.

71

philosopher longs to reach his ultimate perfection, this will come to be if he has already attained both the theoretical and practical sciences and both the moral and cogitative virtues, and especially the greatest of them.

[The term] "king" initially indicates, in [its] primary intention, the one who rules in cities. It is evident that the art by which he controls the governance of cities will be
10 completed only if all these conditions are combined in him. The case of the Lawgiver is also like this. Although this word initially indicates one who has the cogitative virtue by which practical things are brought about in nations and cities, he has need of those [same] conditions. Hence these names are, as it were, synonymous—i.e., "philosopher,"
15 "king," "Lawgiver"; and so also is "Imam," since *imām* in Arabic means one who is followed in his actions. He who is followed in these actions by which he is a philosopher, is an Imam in the absolute sense. As to whether it should be made a condition that he be a prophet, why there is room here for ⌐penetrating⌐ investigation, ⌐and we shall investigate⌐ it in the first part of this science, God willing. Perhaps if this were so, it would be with respect to what is preferable,
20 not out of necessity. As it has already been made clear what   ⌐
the philosopher is, and as it has already been made clear   485–
that only such people as these can be the ruler of this   487a
virtuous city and govern over it, we ought to mention the

61.8-16   Farabi, *Attainment*, 41.17-43.19 (*MPP*, pp. 78 f.); *Virtuous City*, 59.11-13 (Dieterici tr., p. 94). Where Averroes has "Lawgiver," he who lays down the Law, Farabi has "legislator," he who lays down the nomoi.

61.17   penetrating investigation] Averroes' disinclination to commit himself here on this point suggests that one ought not simply to assume as necessarily divinely revealed that *sharī'a* brought by the Lawgiver mentioned a few lines above.

61.22   Compare the following account with Farabi's enumeration in *Attainment*, 44.15-45.9 (*MPP*, p. 80); and *Virtuous City*, 59.14-60.11 (Dieterici tr., pp. 94-96).

qualities that will be found in these chiefs by nature. They
are the natural conditions in a king. One of them—and this
is the most distinctive—is that he be disposed by nature to
the study of the theoretical sciences. This will be if, by his
natural disposition, he can recognize what is essential and
25 distinguish it from what is accidental. The second, that he
be retentive, not forgetful. For it is impossible for anyone
lacking these two qualities to learn anything. That is because he will not cease being always weary to the point that
he abandons learning and reading. The third, that he love
learning and choose it and have a wonderful longing for all
30 parts of science. For as he says, one who longs very much
for a thing will want all of its kinds; for example, the lover
of wine desires all [kinds of] wine, and similarly the lover of
women. The fourth, that he love truth and hate falsehood.
62. For he who loves knowledge of what is, | as such, is a lover
of truth; and he who loves truth cannot be a lover of falsehood; hence he whose way this is, will not be a lover of
falsehood. The fifth, that he despise the sensual desires. For
when someone's desire fixes on something with the utmost
intensity, his soul is deflected from the other desires. Simi-
5 larly with these, since they already incline with all their
⌐souls⌐ toward study. The sixth, that he not be a lover of
money. For [love of] money is a desire, and desires are not
becoming in these people. The seventh, that he be of
enlarged thought. For one who yearns for knowledge of the
whole and of all things that are and does not wish [his]
knowledge of things to be limited to whatever is affirmed
on the basis of unexamined opinion is [indeed] of very
10 enlarged thought. Hence there is no proportion whatever
[of anything] to this cogitative soul. The eighth, that he be
courageous. For one who has no courage will be unable to
despise the nondemonstrative arguments on which he has
grown up, and especially if he has grown up in these cities.

The ninth, that he be so disposed that he moves on his own toward whatever he holds to be good and beautiful, such as justice and the other virtues. This is so if his appetitive soul
15 has firm faith in thought and cogitation.   ⌊

To be added to these is that he be eloquent so that his tongue lead him [to express] whatever is in his ⌈thoughts⌉ while he is speculating. Moreover, he should be able to light quickly upon the middle term.

These, then, are the conditions of the soul that are stipulated for these people. As for the conditions of the body, why they are those very conditions that were stipulated for
20 the guardians with a view to the good and improvement of the physique. He is fit to rule over this city in whom these conditions have been combined from the outset of his being and who, in addition, chanced to grow up in the kind of governance that he [sc., Plato] describes later on. On account of all this, the existence of people such as these is infrequent; and that is the cause of the difficulty [attending] this city's existence. Someone might say: If the existence of
25 this city can only come about if people such as these happen to exist, and their existing with these qualities [is contingent on] their having grown up in this city, why then there is no way in which this city can come into being. What we were laying down ⌈in speech⌉ and had then thought to be possible is [now seen to be] impossible. The answer is that

62.16 eloquent] Averroes has made this a leading theme in his *Decisive Treatise*. Plato's several enumerations of the qualities necessary in a philosopher or guardian or tyrant make no mention of eloquence. (Compare *Republic* 485a–487a, as well as 374e–376c, and *Laws* 709e–710c.) But this does appear in Farabi's enumeration in *Virtuous City*, 59.21, 59.5-6 (Dieterici tr., pp. 95, 94). See also Farabi, *Attainment*, 44.6-13 (*MPP*, pp. 79 f.); and Maimonides, *Guide*, I 34 (41a) (Pines tr., p. 78). The importance of rhetoric in the political science of the *falāsifa* is discussed briefly by Leo Strauss in "Quelques remarques sur la science politique de Maimonide et de Fârâbî," *Revue des Études Juives*, 100 (1936): 37, additional note to p. 26, n. 3.

it is possible for ⌜individuals⌝ to grow up with these natural
qualities that we have attributed to them—developing,
30 moreover, so as to choose the general common nomos that
63. not a single nation can help choosing; | and besides, their
particular Law would not be far from the human Laws;
[if these conditions are fulfilled] wisdom would have been
completed in their time. This is as matters are in this time
of ours and in our Law. If it should happen that the likes of
these come to rule for an infinite time, it is possible for this
5 city to come into being. When it became clear to him ⌜
through argument that this city's existence necessitates that   487c–
those ruling over it be wise, he turned to investigate the   487e
cause on account of which these cities, presently existing,
do not receive any advantage from philosophers and the
wise. He said that this is for two causes. [a] One is because ⌞
10 these cities neither heed the bidding of the wise who are
truly wise nor look to them [for anything]. He said, by way ⌜
                                                                488

62.29-63.1 See 57.29 ("general nomos"), 47.27-28, and 26.16
("human Laws"), above. Consider Aristotle *Nicomachean Ethics* 5. 7.
1134b18-1135a5. Farabi concludes his summary of Book VII of Plato's
Laws with these words: "Then he set out, after that, to explain that
Traditions are of two classes: a class that pertains to the Law of each
one of the legislators according to their need in their times and the
states of their cities; and [the second] Traditions that do not change and
do not alter, and they are natural. He spoke profusely in this connection, and introduced for that examples relating to kindred, ingrat-
itude for favors, and the like" (*Plato's Laws*, 36.15-18). The general
common nomos is something like a natural standard, a set of rules
common to all times and places, without which any kind of lasting
human association would be impossible. It does not aim high. Under
certain special circumstances, under the guidance of qualified leaders,
it is possible for men to go beyond this. They will then come close to the
human Laws. The latter, however, can only be approximated and never
made universal; they are the laws by which philosophers govern
themselves. See Pines, pp. 70 f.; the lengthy analysis in Leo Strauss,
Persecution and the Art of Writing (Glencoe, Ill.: Free Press, 1952),
pp. 95-141; and *International Encyclopedia of the Social Sciences*, s.v. "Natural Law."

of giving a simile: [The relation of] the wise to the citizens
of these cities is like that of a pilot, expert in the science of
navigation, who can find no one to learn it or to make use
of navigation. The sailors assert that navigation is not something that can be taught; nor is it an art entitling its master
to become ruler over the sailors. Rather, if someone says to
them that this art can be taught, they ⌜will despise him⌝
15 and shun him. ⌜Later on⌝ someone who holds this opinion
of navigation comes to be pilot of the ship, either by coercing
the sailors or by something else through which one comes to
power. If the ship is ruled by people such as those, will they
then not turn away from the leader who is truly a leader
and sometimes [even] despise him? Just so is the situation of
the wise in these cities among their citizens. For their rank ├──
20 among them is that of physicians among the sick—[the 489a–
latter] not considering medicine to be the art of healing and 489c
hence not holding the physicians in esteem. If the physicians
tell them ⌜that⌝ they can be healed, they stone them [to
death]. Hence the work of the medical art will not be
perfected unless the sick are fully bound to and do submit to
the physicians. For whoever is ill undoubtedly needs to go
25 to the physicians' doors, ⌜as he says⌝. Such is the situation └─
of the wise among the citizens. This, then, is one cause why
citizens today receive no advantage from the wise who are
truly wise. [*b*] The second cause is the defectiveness of most
of those giving themselves to wisdom, if they lack [even] one
of those qualities that we said were conditions of the wise
one who is truly wise. It is rare that there is one in whom ┌─
these qualities exist to perfection; and even when he is to be 491
30 found it is with difficulty ⌜that this knowledge—i.e.,⌝ philosophy—is perfected in him. Those virtuous qualities are,
64. of all things, what most hinder | many of those growing up

63.19-24   See also Averroes, *Decisive Treatise*, 22.21-23.1 (*MPP*,
p. 182).

in these cities from [pursuing] philosophy. The case here is
like the case of many of the sick whose disease is aggravated
by excellent food. Similarly, if the proper place and nutri-
ment are not found for them, the seeds of the best plants
will turn into the very worst of the bad kinds. Such is the
5 case with these virtuous natures when they grow up in these
cities and are badly educated. Hence the causes of the great
evils in these cities are none other than these ⌐individuals⌐.
For the sluggish nature cannot be aroused to perform something great; similarly, the ⌐mean-⌐spirited; while the intem-
perate is even further from this. From this class of humans
10 originate the sophists who rule over cities, blaming the
beautiful things such as wisdom and the rest, and praising
the base things and in general all the political evils laid
down in cities. Their thought and their rulership over the
cities: this indeed is the greatest of the causes for the loss of
wisdom and the extinguishing of its light. In investigating
such individuals as these, let it not be hidden from you that
they constitute the larger portion [of the virtuous natures]
in these cities. If, nonetheless, one of these natures in these
cities is saved, and you said that it is God who singled him
out through His ⌐eternal⌐ providence, you would have made
15 a correct statement. As for those given over to philosophy
without these qualities having been completed in them, why
the case with them is also evident. Not only does one receive
no advantage from them in cities, but they are also the most
harmful of things for wisdom. That is because for the most
part they incline one way—toward the desires and toward
base actions in general, like violence and oppression. For

64.7-8   mean-spirited] Literally: the small-souled.
64.16-22   On philosophizing by those who are not ready for it, see
Ibn Ṭufayl, *Ḥayy*, p. 155 (*MPP*, p. 161); and Averroes, *Decisive Treatise*,
5.19-22, 17.15-20, 18.7-10 (*MPP*, pp. 168, 178). Much of Farabi's
discussion of the "weeds" in virtuous cities is apposite here (*Political
Regime*, 104.7-107.19 [*MPP*, pp. 53-56]).

20 they have no virtue in and of themselves that would restrain
them from these actions; nor will they speak truly in the
tales with which they frighten the citizens ⌜while bringing
about these things⌝ [sc., violence and the like]. They will be
a disgrace to wisdom and a cause of much harm to whichever of them is fit for it, as is the case in this time of ours. If ⌜
it happens that a true philosopher grows up in these cities,   496d–
he is in the position of a man who has come among perilous   497a
animals. He is not obliged to do harm along with them, but
25 neither is he sure in himself that those animals will not
oppose him. Hence he turns to isolation and lives the life of
a solitary. The best perfection is missing in him, for that can
be attained by him only in this city that we have described
in speech.   ⌞

It has become evident from this statement what the nature of the philosopher is, and because of what we adjudge
the name "philosopher" [to someone], and that there is no
65. way of saving the cities unless | people such as these rule
over them. With this the cause why it is difficult for this city
to come into being has become evident, and [also] how it
happens that this nature [sc., the philosophic nature] is
accidentally harmful. It is now fitting that we return to the
manner of educating this particular kind—namely the
ruling kind—in this city. There is no way of understanding
5 the correctness in their education and upbringing unless it
is known what end this kind of humans strive for in their
governance. We hold it to be indispensable that we know
this first. [Only] then is it possible for us to speak of the

64.23-26 Avempace, *Governance*, 11.9-14, 78.6-12 (*MPP*, pp. 128,
132); Ibn Ṭufayl, *Ḥayy*, pp. 153 f. (*MPP*, pp. 160 f.); Maimonides,
Guide, II 36 (79b) (Pines tr., p. 372).

64.28 In the ensuing discussion (64.28-74.12), Averroes moves away
from an exposition that relies in any obvious way on Plato's text. The
corresponding passage in the *Republic* is 497b–511e, where among other
things the discussion is of the ideas and the divided line.

details of that in which they are to be educated. For he who
does not know the end necessarily cannot know what leads
to it. Although this investigation would be ⌜more⌝ appropriate in the first part of this science, I deem it appropriate
that I mention some of it here.

10   We say: Since man is one of the natural beings there
necessarily must be some end for the sake of which he
exists. For every natural being has an end, as has been
explained in physics—all the more so man, who is the most
noble of them. Since the city is necessary for man's existence,
he can attain this end only inasmuch as he is part of a city.
It is evident that this end, inasmuch as it pertains to one
15   being, is necessarily one. [This will be] either [a] in kind—so
that it belongs to each and every one of the people, as far as
number is concerned, this being what we see of the end,
which whether sufficiently or insufficiently, is one in number; or [b] in relationship—i.e., if many perfections are for
the sake of one perfection and some of them for the sake of
others—for this is one in that the many things by it are
[made] one. If man is not of more than one kind, and if the
20   human perfections are manifold in this aspect of existence,
and if it were possible that all of them be attained by all
people, why it is evident that every one of the people would
exist only for his own sake. Accordingly, it would be necessary that there would be only one rank of humans in a city.
Perhaps this is impossible. If the attainment of all or most
of them [sc., the human perfections] is possible for only some
people, while nature limits the others to something different
than the fulfillment of the perfections, it is evident that the

65.13-14   Medigo (apparently reading *medīnī* rather than *ha-medīnah*)
translates: But because man, from the necessity of his being, is political,
that end comes to him inasmuch as he is part of a city.

65.23-26   Farabi, *Political Regime*, 74.3-75.3, 78.1-79.9, 83.11-84.9
(*MPP*, pp. 35 f., 39).

25 second kind of humans are lorded over and the first kind
lord it. For their relationship to each other is identical with
the relationship of those very perfections ⌜in⌝ the individual
soul—i.e., that some of them are for the sake of others. The
things that humans may possibly consider as the end are
undoubtedly infinite, but of this we ourselves will only
specify what is generally accepted in this time of ours.

We say: [a] [Some] humans ⌜assert⌝ that the end of man
30 is nothing more than preserving and protecting their bodies
and preserving their senses. Their association is solely a
⌜necessity-⌝association, and their end that they ⌜aim⌝ at is
a "necessary" end. [b] Others assert that it is not appropriate
66. for man | to be limited in his existence to what is necessary;
rather, he has an end that has something better in it than
existence at the level of the necessary. This is in accord with
what is the case with many of the natural beings. For an
animal is given sight for the sake of what is preferable, not
on account of necessity—contrary to the case regarding the
sense of touch, for it is impossible for an animal to exist
5 without this sense. The people who hold this opinion concerning the end of man are divided into parts: [1] [some]
humans ⌜hold⌝ that it is wealth; [2] [other] people hold
that it is honor; [3] [still] others assert that it is pleasure.
Those who hold that it is pleasure are divided into two
parts: [a'] [some] humans assert that it is the delight of the
senses (they are closer to unexamined opinion); and [b']
others think that it is the delight of the intelligible. [4]
Others assert that the end of man is only that he lord it
10 over others and rule them, while acquiring all the goods of
pleasure, wealth, honor, and whatever else they assert to be
[desirable]. [5] What the Laws existing in this time of ours

65.29-31   For the necessity-association or the indispensable association, see Farabi, *Political Regime*, 88.4-13 (*MPP*, pp. 42 f.); and
Virtuous City, 62.4-6 (Dieterici tr., p. 98).

assert concerning this matter is [that the end of man is doing] what God (may He be exalted!) wills, but that the only ⌜way⌝ of knowing this matter of what it is God wills of them is prophecy. And this [sc., what God wills], if you reflect on the Laws, is divided into abstract knowledge

15 alone—such as what our Law commands concerning knowledge of God (may He be exalted!)—and action— such as what it forewarns concerning the [moral] qualities. Its intention regarding this purpose [sc., action] is identical with the intention of philosophy in genus and purpose. That is why humans assert that these Laws only follow ancient wisdom. It is evident that, in the opinion of all these, the good, the bad, the useful, the harmful, the beautiful, and the base are something existing by nature, not by convention. For whatever leads to the end is good

20 and beautiful, and whatever hinders one from it is bad and base. This is clear from these Laws and particularly this Law of ours. Many of those of our region hold ⌜this opinion concerning this Law of ours⌝.

As for the people of our ⌜nation⌝ known as Mutakallimūn, their Legal inquiry led them to [the position] that what God wills has no definite nature and merely turns on what the will—i.e., the will of God (may He be exalted!)—lays down for it. According to this, there is nothing beautiful or

25 base other than by fiat. Furthermore, there is no end of man other than by fiat. What brought them to this was their thinking of defending the attributes with which God (may He be exalted!) is described in the Law, to the effect that

66.15   commands] MS *A* adds: us.
66.21   The reference is to the Muʻtazilites, who hold that the Law prescribes what is according to nature or reason.
66.22   our nation] MS *A*: our faith.
66.23   Legal inquiry] I.e., theorizing from the standpoint of the Law. See Averroes, *Decisive Treatise*, 1.7 (*MPP*, p. 165).

He is capable of doing whatever He wills, and that it is
possible for the [divine] will to extend to all things, including
particulars as well. Hence all things are possible. What
happened to them happens often in Legal inquiry. That is,
30 God (may He be exalted!) is first described by [certain]
attributes. Then one seeks to make what exists agree [with
the teaching] without ⌐upsetting⌐ whatever of those attributes has been laid down. But these [people] are distressed
in [trying] to discover the explanation of this question if
these things that they consider clearly evident in the Law
67. are as they believe. As a result this leads them | to an
opinion close to sophistry, very far from the nature of man,
and far from being the content of a Law. These, then, are
the opinions of the multitude concerning the end of man,
which is his happiness. The realization of their absurdity is
readily grasped. As for the opinions of the philosophers, we
shall mention them when we come to investigate that where-
5 in they differ since their controversy is ⌐only⌐ over the
rational part of the soul. We return to the subject under
consideration and investigate the end that is truly the end
after accepting what ought to be accepted from the physicist
concerning this, for thereby we perceive the proper measure
of what can be seen of this through this science.

   We say that he who possesses this science joins with the

66.28   particulars as well] Other MSS: It extends only to particulars.

   67.1   Averroes, *Decisive Treatise*, 23.19-24.13, 25.18-19 (*MPP*,
pp. 183 f., 185); Maimonides, *Guide*, I 71 (95ab, 97b), 73, tenth premise
(112b-114b) (Pines tr., pp. 178 f., 182, 206-209). See 30.26-29, above.

   67.4   The opinions of the philosophers are here distinguished from
all of the foregoing—i.e., not only from the views of the dialectical
theologians, but from all of the opinions catalogued since 65.29. From
this standpoint, all of the foregoing opinions are "generally accepted,"
endoxa, "opinions of the multitude."

   67.8   For the themes of the following excursus (continuing to 74.12),
see Aristotle *Physics* 2. 1-2. 192b-194b, 8. 198b-199a, 3. 1. 200b-201b;
De Anima 2. 1-4. 412a-415b, 3. 5. 430a, 9-11. 432a-434a; *Nicomachean*

physicist in inquiry concerning this object of search. For
10 physics considers this end in so far as it is a perfection for
the body and compares it with the other perfections if there
be more than one perfection for it. As for the human perfections, nothing ⌜of them⌝ exists by nature save the dispositions alone or the beginnings leading to their [sc., the
perfections'] attainment. There is no sure sufficiency in
nature that these completions will reach us in their perfection; rather, they reach [us] only through will and
15 skillfulness. He who possesses this science also considers it
from this aspect—i.e., from the aspect that its efficient cause
is choice and will. This being so, I say that it has already
been made clear in physics that man is composed of soul
and body; and that the rank of the body relative to the soul
is that of matter, and the rank of the soul relative to it is
that of form; and that matter is for the sake of form, and the
form is for the sake of the actions or the passions resulting
from it [sc., the form]. This being so, man's perfection and
end are to be found in the actions that necessarily result
20 from it [sc., the soul]. But it has been explained there that
the actions pertaining to man are [of two kinds]: Either [*a*]
they are common to ⌜him⌝ and to other natural beings, be
they simple or compound ([these] common [actions] necessarily resulting from common forms); or [*b*] they are specifi-
cally his (these necessarily resulting from a specific form or
forms). It was explained there that the thing that man has
in common with the simple bodies is the faculty of incli-
25 nation. The inclination resulting from this faculty in this
form is not a soul, nor do the actions resulting from it belong
to the soul. As for what man has in common with the
compound bodies, why it was explained there that it neces-

Ethics 1. 1. 1094a, 7. 1097a–1098a, 13. 1102a–1103a, 3. 2. 1111b-1112a, 6. 1-2. 1139ab, 10. 6-7. 1176a-1178a. "Physics," as used here, refers broadly to natural science.

sarily is a soul. These bodies are of two kinds: plants and animals. The plants have in common with him the nutritive,
30 vegetative, and generative soul. As for the animals, they have in common with him the faculties of sensation and locomotion. As for the appetitive [faculties], they have them in common with him in certain respects and are set apart
68. from him in other respects. | As for what distinguishes man, it was made evident there that it is necessarily the ⌜rational⌝ faculty, and that this has two parts—practical reason and scientific reason. It was also made evident there that the rank of these common forms relative to the specific forms is that of matter relative to form; and that man is what he is only on account of his specific form since this is the way with every being. For it is through its specific form that it is what
5 it is, and from it result the actions that are specific to it. This having been laid down, the good and bad in a thing exist in only one class of its actions. An example of this is that a melody's good [quality] only comes from striking a chord and its bad [quality] from this very action. [In the same way] the good and bad of a man's action are necessarily to be found only in the action specific ⌜to him⌝. This being so, a man's end and happiness [are attained] only if those of his
10 actions that are specific to him are realized by him in the utmost goodness and excellence. That is why it is said in the definition of happiness that it is an activity of the rational soul that is in accord with what is required by virtue. And since the parts of the rational soul—in accord with what has been explained there—are more than one, the virtues are of more than one kind and the ⌜human⌝ perfections are of more than one perfection. For it has been explained there that it has two parts, practical reason and scientific reason.
15 Some perfections, accordingly, are theoretical and others practical. But since the appetitive part is one of the parts of the soul, it comes about that man is aroused by what inquiry

requires of him and is connected with it. In this respect, too,
it [sc., the appetitive part] is related to reason. There are,
then, three perfections: theoretical virtues, moral virtues,
and practical ⌜arts⌝. But the practical ⌜arts⌝ are of two
20 kinds. One kind, in order to realize its actions in matter,
needs nothing more than knowledge of the general rules of
the art. The [other] kind additionally needs for the existence
of its actions cogitation and thought about the general rules
with which it is associated. For since this [takes place] with
each and every individual affected by the art and according
to the time, place, ⌜and the rest⌝ connected with it, this
part of reason necessarily differs from the other part, and
its perfection is not [the other's] perfection. The perfections,
25 then, are four: theoretical virtues, practical ⌜arts⌝, cogitative virtues, and moral virtues. It is already seen from this
argument that the human perfections are more than one.
But as we have said, if they are perfections of only one being,
then of necessity some of them must be for the sake of others;
[and this] regardless of whether their existence is possible in
all individual men or it is only possible for some [of these
perfections to be found] in some and leaving aside the fact
that it is evident that they are not possible in all individual
30 humans. Each [particular] kind of them is only possible in
[some particular] class of people, except ⌜—by God!—⌝ for
some of the moral virtues, which are common [to all], like
moderation. ⌜Hence⌝ it is obligatory that these classes of
people be arranged in accord with the order of these kinds
69. of moral virtues, | the meaner of them being for the sake of
the more excellent, since the character of their order in a
particular individual will be the same as their order in many
individuals. This conforms with what the necessity of association brings about in human existence: [namely those]

68.18   three perfections] See 22.9-11, above.
68.27   See 65.23-26, above.

who excel in all the virtues. For if there were in every
5 individual the possibility of attaining all these virtues—each
and every one of them necessarily attaining them—each
would be serving and served, lord and lorded over. Nature
would have done something in vain since they all would
have the disposition to be lords. This is impossible since of
necessity a lord must have someone there who is lorded over.

If it were possible for these perfections to be combined in
one man, this would be considered difficult if not miracu-
lous. The usual situation is that each and every kind of
10 human ⌜is disposed⌝ toward some particular one of these
perfections. This is clear from investigation of individual
humans. It has been explained what the human perfections
and the virtues of the soul are; and it has been made clear
as well that some of them are required for the sake of others,
so that there will be a virtue among them for whose sake all
these [other] virtues are, while it will not be for the sake of
anything else, being rather the thing sought for itself and
the rest being sought for it. This is man's ultimate perfection
15 and ultimate happiness. Hence it is fitting that we investigate it.

We say: It appears from the case of the practical arts that
they were originally established only because of necessity
due to ⌜the deficiency⌝ that is incidental to man's existence.
His existence would not be possible without them, just as
the existence of many of the animals would not be possible
but for their peculiarities and natural habits, such as the
20 hexagonal cell of the bee and the weaving of the spider. As
for the theoretical part, it appears in physics from its
character that its existence in man is not because of necessity
but rather for the sake of what is preferable. Whatever
exists for the sake of what is preferable is more choiceworthy
than whatever exists because of necessity. Hence this part
of reason—i.e., the practical—exists necessarily for the sake

of the theoretical. This conforms with what can be seen of
25 its character. For it is evident that these arts only exist
initially for the sake of their products, and their products
for the sake of justice. Now by virtue of his acquiring these
arts, a man is necessarily lorded over and subject, and
⌐someone else¬ is the lord. The lord will be lord by a disposition in him by [virtue of] which he is better than the one
being lorded over. This being so, this disposition is nothing
other than the part of reason called theoretical. For the
manner in which this part of reason lords it over the ⌐other¬
30 part—i.e., the practical—in the particular soul is identical
with the manner in which one who is disposed to receive
the theoretical sciences lords it [over anyone] whose natural
disposition is sufficient for [only] the practical arts. Hence
70.   the likes of these serve ⌐by nature¬ | and are lorded over
⌐by nature¬. For the relationship of one of these two parts
of the soul to the other part is ⌐necessarily¬ this relationship
—i.e., the relation of the lord to the one being lorded over.
It is possible to question this by saying: These practical arts
have been laid down, all leading up to one ruling art—
namely the art of governing cities. It also has been made
5 clear that the theoretical sciences are necessary for this art's
existence. ⌐This being so, the theoretical sciences¬ are only
preparations with a view to action. Through them [sc., the
theoretical sciences] a man benefits others. There is no
difference between them [sc., the theoretical sciences] and
the other, practical arts other than that [the practical arts]
serve them in attaining their [sc., the theoretical sciences']
intention. And they [sc., the practical arts] grant them lordship in that they [sc., the theoretical sciences] prepare them
[sc., the practical arts] with a view to their [sc., the
theoretical sciences'] purpose. [Thus the theoretical sciences
are] in the position of the other ruling arts with respect to
10 the arts that grant them lordship—such as the ruling art of

agriculture with respect to the particular agricultural [arts] beneath it. Accordingly, the theoretical sciences and the practical arts belong to one genus and differ only in inferiority and excellence. This is the opinion asserted perhaps by many of the pretenders to philosophy of this time of ours from among those who direct [their] inquiry to those things —[their inquiry] being based on unexamined opinion without their considering them according to the natural order and the study [done by rules of] art.

15 We say: That concerning which the theoretical sciences speculate, and particularly physics and metaphysics, are not practical things; nor has the will any effect upon their existence. This is self-evident to one who is trained in sciences such as these. This being so, and the subjects of these sciences being such that their being is not up to us, it is clear that they are not disposed toward action [by their] primary disposition and essentially. Through them a man
20 does not—as the primary intention— serve others. Rather their existence in man is with respect to what is preferable, for it would be absurd if their existence in man were null and in vain. This can be seen better from what we are about to say. It has already been made clear in first philosophy that being is of two kinds: sensible and intelligible. Intelligible being is the principle of sensible existence in
25 that it is its end, form, and efficient cause. Its [sc., the sensible's] existence in the intelligibles of the theoretical sciences belongs to the class of intelligible ⌐existence⌐. The purpose of man, inasmuch as he is a natural being, is that he ascend to that existence as much as it is in his nature to ascend. This being so, the relation of this ⌐human⌐ intelligible existence ⌐to the other things existing in man, be they soul or body, is the relation of intelligible existence⌐, simply,

70.23 Aristotle *Metaphysics* 7. 10. 1036a2-12, 8. 6. 1045a33-36.
70.29 I.e., in that it is its end, form, and efficient cause.

30 to sensible existence. Similarly, in so far as it is acquired by
the will, its relation to the other volitional things is the very
71. same relation. | This being presupposed, its lordship over
the volitional things consists in the primacy of intelligible
existence over ⌜sensible⌝ existence, and in its giving the
volitional beings their principles on which their existence
depends—this by way of the intelligible existence giving the
5 sensible existence what it depends on. It has already been
made clear that this is not by way of the intelligible's serving
the sensible; rather it [sc., the sensible] is something that
follows on it [sc., the intelligible] and is necessitated by it.
This being so, the theoretical sciences are indeed useful for
action and necessary for action in the way in which it is
said of intelligible existence that it is necessary for sensible
existence. The primacy of this part over the other parts of
the city resembles the primacy of intelligible existence over
10 sensible existence. It may be seen from this treatise that the
practical arts—be they faculties, or ruling or ministerial
arts—exist only because of the theoretical sciences. People
have asserted ⌜an opinion⌝ concerning the existence of these
practical arts that—upon my life!—is just the opposite of
what these assert concerning the theoretical sciences. For
they say that the intelligibles of these arts are not—according to the primary intention—for the sake of their products,
but [rather] that their sole purpose is good and excellent
15 discernment; and that the actions and products resulting
from them are something incidental. [This would be of] the
order of what appears in the case of the movements of the
heavenly bodies. Accordingly, the practical arts are the
virtues [simply]. Even more is this thought of those practical

71.5-6 In a way the higher may serve the lower, but in fact it is not
service. The sensible is posterior to the intelligible.
71.9 over sensible existence] MS *A* adds: or over existence simply.
71.17-18 See 68.19-21, above, for the two kinds of practical arts.

arts that make use of reasoning. As for these positive qualities resulting from these arts, it is thought by those who
20 ⌜concentrate⌝ on a single art that that art encompasses
knowledge of all things, as ⌜we see⌝ the physicians ⌜think-
ing⌝ of their art. But the truth is that the intelligibles of
these ⌜arts⌝ were established at first only with a view to
activity; if one perceives anything by them, it is by accident.
If, therefore, the perceiving is put down as the end of the
art, it [sc., the art] would belong to another genus. The term
["art"] applied to them would be said homonymously, just
as happens to the term "music," which is defined sometimes
as the practical art and sometimes as the theoretical one.
25 As for the cogitative virtues, it is evident from their case
too that they are for the sake of the theoretical intelligibles.
For the existence of these virtues is mostly—⌜or⌝ the existence of the noblest of them [is universally]—for the sake of
the arts; and the arts, as has been explained in this treatise,
are for the sake of the theoretical intelligibles. For it is
evident that these cogitative virtues are divided as the arts
30 are divided. Just as there is an art ⌜unqualifiedly⌝ ruling
over all the arts—namely the art of governing cities—so is
there a ruling cogitative faculty—namely the faculty by
which the actions of this [ruling] art are materialized. |

72. As for the moral virtues, it appears from their case too
that they are for the sake of the theoretical intelligibles.
And this is for several reasons: One of them, as has already
been made clear in physics, is that appetite and desire are
of two kinds: one stems from the imagination, and the other
stems from cogitation and thought. The appetite that stems
from the imagination is of necessity not specific to man,
5 being rather connected with the animal as animal. As for
the appetite that stems from cogitation and thought, why it

71.25 The theme of this brief paragraph is developed at length in
Farabi, *Attainment*, 20.3-29.7 (*MPP*, pp. 64-69).

is specific to man; and the existence of appetite of this
character is connected with man. The moral virtues are
nothing other than that this part of us is aroused toward
that which cogitation judges ought to come into being, to
10 the extent that it judges and at the time that it judges. It is
evident that this activity belongs to nothing other than the
theoretical part of the soul. This being so, it is ⌜only⌝ this
part that acquires virtue from the cogitative part. The
cogitative part, then, is more truly elevated; it is ⌜more⌝
noble and more choiceworthy. Also many of the animals
have a share in this [moral] part—such as the modesty to be
found in the lion—but it is human only by virtue of thought
15 and cogitation, and whatever is the cause of something's
being of a certain character possesses that character to a
higher degree. It can also be seen now from the case of these
virtues that through them a man serves others. For example,
justice exists only because of [reciprocal] dealings, moderation because of pleasures that hinder noble actions, courage
because of harmful things, and liberality because of wealth.
But as for theoretical science, why it is ⌜clear⌝ from its
20 character that a man is not disposed toward it that he might
serve others. Moreover, these virtues are more apt to be
hylic than the theoretical sciences and more apt to be in
need of the body for their continued existence—and not
only of the body, but also of instruments and external
things. Thus liberality has need of wealth so that, by means
of it, it might perform acts of liberality; similarly the just
performs acts of justice through them [sc., instruments];
25 and the courageous has need of strength and help. But as

72.13-14   The example of the lion is given by Avempace, *Governance*,
55.14 (Asín tr., p. 93).

72.21   hylic] I.e., material or grounded in matter.

72.24   Liberality thus needs wealth in two respects—as something
to be overcome (72.18-19), and as an indispensable means.

for the theoretical sciences, they are of all things the strongest, the most free of matter, to the point that they are thought to be in a manner everlasting. It has already been made clear elsewhere that the more strongly separated something is from hyle, the more noble it is. But this kind ⌐of perfection—i.e.⌐, the moral, is laid down [in relation to]
30 theoretical perfection as a preparatory rank, without which the attainment of the end is impossible. Hence this perfection is thought to be the ultimate end because of its proximity to the ultimate end. It appears from this, then, that the human perfections are of four classes and that they are all for the sake of theoretical perfection. |

73.   As to whether the moral virtues are for the sake of the practical arts or vice versa, or whether both cases exist together—i.e., that some arts are for the sake of the virtues and some virtues for the sake of the arts—why there is room in this for ⌐penetrating⌐ investigation. But it is clear that the ruling moral virtue of all these virtues must neces-
5 sarily be joined to the ruling cogitative faculty. If the ruling virtue's relation to the ruling cogitative faculty is as the relation of the cogitative faculty to the ruling art, why then it necessarily is for the sake of the ruling art. Just so is the case with those arts to which no kind of this virtue belongs.
10 For in accord with this relation, it—i.e., the practical arts— is only laid down as a preparatory rank. ⌐Though⌐ their [sc., the moral virtues'] acquisition is necessary for it [sc., the art], it is only so that the activity of the art may be more perfect and more praiseworthy. This is self-evident. But however the case may be here, both of them together are for the sake of the theoretical part. What we have said concerning the analogies between these human perfections
15 is an agreed-upon thing among the Peripatetics. But as this

73.5-7   See 70.3-4 and 71.30-32, above.

theoretical part does not exist in us from the outset in its
ultimate perfection and in actuality, its existence in us is
only potential. It has been made clear in physics that everything that has potentiality in its existence or has potentiality
mixed in its existence [can attain] its ultimate perfection
only when it exists as complete actuality with no potentiality
at all mixed with it. It is for us to bring into being and to
perfect the perfection and actuality that are of this character
20 —i.e., it comes to pass through choice and will since there
is no sufficiency in nature to bring it about. What then is
this perfection that it is incumbent upon us to pursue and
which is the end that we would realize in ourselves? Is it the
theoretical sciences, or another rank and another creation
more noble than the theoretical sciences? If it is other than
the theoretical sciences, is it something found in us or something that ⌜in its substance is outside ourselves?⌝

25 We say: As for him who assumes that the theoretical
sciences are everlasting and that they exist in us in actuality
and that the humors have only submerged them since youth,
why in this manner they are as if they stood still in potential
existence. Either they are separate forms, as Plato assumes,
or it is the Active Intellect or an intellect other than that
and beneath it in rank. It is evident that [if this is assumed]
human perfection is not itself acquired through the will
30 since it exists in its essence prior to the will. [Yet] will is
connected with its definition inasmuch as it ⌜has a connec-
tion⌝ with the definition of the ultimate perfections. In this
respect it is taken as a ⌜premise⌝ for the definition of the
74. end. | If it be said that this is only something acquired by
us by will—i.e., when we acquire of the other ultimate

73.25-31 Farabi, *Political Regime*, 71.10-72.14, 79.9-11 (*MPP*, pp.
33 f., 36). See also Averroes' summary of Aristotle's *De Anima* (*Talkhīṣ
kitāb al-nafs*, ed. Aḥmad Fuʾād al-Ahwānī [Cairo, 1950], 66.9-10,
72.13-73.7).

perfections whatever is in our nature to acquire—that perfection [nonetheless] would [still] reach us through that relationship by [virtue of] whose connection to us we are what we are. For it is known that if this acquisition is related to the will, it is only related in ways other than the
5 former ways since will is not connected with that by which we realize ourselves. Rather, will is connected with the existence of the relationship ⌐by which⌐ the Active Intellect achieves our perfection. As for him who asserts that the theoretical sciences are not everlasting but that they are the ultimate perfection, why human perfection according to him would be what the will itself acquires. As for him who holds that ⌐the theoretical⌐ sciences are not everlasting and that the ultimate perfection is having a conception of
10 the separate intelligences, why it is evident that perfection according to him [would consist of] two kinds: a first and a final [perfection]. The first is what he himself acquires; the second is what he acquires through conjunction [with the Active Intellect]. This needs to be investigated in [the study of the soul in] physics. We return to what we were about and ⌐go into each point⌐ of what Plato said about the way of educating this class of people.

We say that Plato compares the relation of this kind of ⌐
15 people, as regards their knowledge, to the rest of the mul- 514
titude. He says that the multitude resemble humans who have lived in a cave since childhood, never having left it. They turn to look carefully at what is in the cave without turning their faces to the mouth of the cave. At the cave's mouth there are images of the other kinds of beings, and at their backs ⌐a fire⌐, so that they see nothing of those ⊢
images other than their shadow on the hollow of the cave. 515

74.11   Aristotle *Physics* 7. 3. 247b1 ff.
74.16-18   Missing here are the references in Plato 514a-515b to prison, prisoners, and chains.

20 This being their situation, these grasp nothing of the knowledge of things other than the shadow of ⌜an image of⌝ beings
falling on the hollow of that cave. They think that true
beings are nothing more than those ⌜shadows⌝. As for the
wise, why they are those who go out to the cave's mouth,
into the sparkling light, and see things as they truly are in
the sunlight. Just as a man who suddenly goes forth from ⊢—
a cave into the sunlight finds that his eyes are grown dim 516ab
25 and that it is impossible for him to look at something, so is
it impossible for this class of humans—i.e., those who are
disposed to knowledge—that we rush them to inquiry in
the sciences since they find it hard to abstract the intelligible
and to look at it. The cunning device adopted with them is
to lead them upward gradually step by step so as to look at
things, first by means of the light of the stars and the moon,
to the point that they are able to look at them in the
presence of the sun. Just so ought the latter to be led upward
gradually step by step, and we direct them [at first] to what ⊢—
75. is easiest for them to learn. | When he investigated which 521d–
science it is that they ⌜ought to⌝ begin [their] study with, it 522c
became clear to him that it was arithmetic. This is because
from the outset they, with the guardians' children, had been
growing up on music and gymnastic. Now it is clear that

74.23 cave's mouth] Other MSS: go out from that cave.

74.24 Plato 515c–516a speaks of the released prisoners being compelled to stand up and face the mouth of the cave and, despite their
protests, being forcibly dragged into sunlight. Farabi's use of the simile
of the cave appears in an excerpt preserved in Shemtob Falqēra, *Moreh
ha-moreh* (Pressburg, 1837; reprint ed., Jerusalem, 5721/1961), 132.12-23
(commentary to Maimonides, *Guide*, III 51). The passage is summarized
and discussed in Leo Strauss, *Philosophie und Gesetz* (Berlin: Schocken
Verlag, 1935), p. 116.

75.1 In the ensuing discussion (75.1-77.13), Averroes again moves
away from Plato's text. At a few points he alights, so to speak, on the
Republic, omitting 516c–521b (what it behooves the philosopher to do
in the Platonic city as contrasted with "these cities") and 531d–537a
(dialectic).

the intention in gymnastic is toward the body. But as for
music, why the statements by which they transmitted this
5 to them are stories, and a story does not grant this faculty— ⌊
i.e., that by which a man can take in the intelligibles of the
theoretical sciences. This being so, this science ought necessarily to be of the class of the theoretical sciences and be
the ⌜easiest⌝ of the mathematical studies. Of this description
are the four mathematical sciences—arithmetic, geometry,
astronomy, and music—except that it [sc., arithmetic] excels
10 in this respect—i.e., ease of study—owing to ⌜its greater⌝
freedom from matter. Arithmetic is then the easiest of them
and that most ⌜common⌝ to all things. It is then followed by
geometry, then astronomy, then music. It is clear from the
character of these sciences that the initial need of the wise
for mathematical sciences is mainly ⌜training⌝, for most of
their intelligibles [sc., of the mathematical sciences] do not
exist as nature intends [natural beings to exist]. Hence there
15 is to be found among them that which has no end. In
general, their intelligibles are defective intelligibles since
they are not conceived of in their particular objects but in
what imitates them. Hence Plato divides the intelligibles ⌈
⌜of⌝ things into two parts. One of them he calls ⌜direct⌝; 533b–
these are the intelligibles of things that truly are. And the 533d
second [he calls thought]; these are the intelligibles of the
appearances of existing things—and they are the mathematical sciences. For he asserts that the case with the intelligibles
20 is like the case with the sensibles. Just as with the sensibles
⌜there are⌝ sensibles that are perceived through their es-
sences and sensibles that are perceived through their

75.7   this science] I.e., the introductory science by which the cave
dwellers are gradually led to see in the light of day.
75.14   as nature intends] Farabi, *Attainment*, 10.2-5 (Mahdi tr.,
p. 19).
75.18   thought] MSS: knowledge. The reference is to Plato's *dianoia*.

appearances (just as what is perceived of many of the
sensibles is their ⌜reflection⌝ in a mirror), so is the case
with the intelligibles. Since, as we have said, the insights
of the mathematical sciences are infinite and their subjects
also of an unknown [manner of] being, only he who pos-
25 sesses First Philosophy investigates them. Plato asserts of
them that they are not of the rank of the other theoretical
sciences as regards human perfection. Hence he says of them ⌊
that they are sciences whose beginnings are unknown and
whose ends are unknown; and [only] what is between the
beginnings and the ends is known. This being so, the
mathematical sciences are not intended initially and essentially for human perfection, as is the case with physics and
30 metaphysics. Although they differ in this respect—and
particularly in what these two sciences take from them
[sc., the mathematical sciences] by way of principles for
the investigation of the end (as when ⌜the⌝ divine science
[sc., metaphysics] accepts the number of movements from
astronomy)—this difference is not only with respect to their
kinds, but also exists with respect to the parts of the partic-
76. ular science. | It is evident that the greater part of the
advantage in them and of what is intended in them at the
outset is only the training and preparation of the intellect
for the study of those two ultimate sciences. We ourselves
are unable to say that what is intended in these sciences—
i.e., the mathematical sciences—is ⌜only⌝ action. [And this]
notwithstanding that some of their students do ⌜somewhat⌝
5 [engage in action]—as many of the multitude think concerning geometry and harmonics. For the things into which
they inquire are common to natural matters and artificial
matters. For example, when it is found that an equilateral
triangle must necessarily have its three sides come out of
the two centers of two equal circles and its two sides resting

76.5   common] I.e., in the sense of being in a border zone.

on the base meet at the point where the two circles intersect,
10 it is nothing peculiar to a triangle existing in wood or copper
or in artificial things generally. It comprises [both] natural
and artificial things. Furthermore, the individual objects
presupposed by these sciences are to be found only in matter.
If the inquiry of these sciences were into that in which they
[sc., geometrical figures] exist, it would investigate their
four causes—i.e., the matter, the form, the efficient cause,
and the end. But it is evident from their case that they
15 investigate the formal cause alone. Hence, they [sc., mathe-
maticians] need individual objects which are included in
these sciences; while engaged in their work, [they need]
knowledge supplementary to what is known by them from
these [sc., mathematical sciences]. If someone wishes to
construct an equilateral triangle out of wood, it is not
enough ⌜for him⌝ [to know] what Euclid said in the beginning of his book on the construction of the equilateral
triangle, without joining to this the craft of carpentry. This
20 is entirely self-evident to one trained in these sciences. All
this being as we have characterized it, the object in teaching
this kind of humans the mathematical sciences is initially
and essentially for the sake of training; though there also is
joined to this, as Plato says, knowledge of the necessary
practices with which they practice them. Inasmuch as they
are guardians, they ⌜also⌝ have need of the knowledge of
25 number and measurements for the array of people in battles,
proper ⌜maneuvers⌝, and the measurements for pitching
camps. Similarly, knowledge of the seasons and months is
also necessary, not only for navigators and those travelling
in deserts, but also for generals. Practical music is necessary
for them in that they are the ones who institute it in the
city. This, then, is what Plato mentions that they begin by
30 studying. He asserts this thought only because the art of

526d, 527d

76.25   maneuvers] Literally: permutations.

logic was nonexistent in his time. But as it ⌐now⌐ exists, it is
proper that they begin their study with the art of logic;
77.   after that | going on ⌐to arithmetic, then⌐ to geometry, then
to astronomy, then to music, then to optics, then to me-
chanics, then to physics, then to metaphysics. However, the
ancients were divided over whether it was obligatory to
5   begin with the art of logic or with the art of mathematics.
Some asserted that logic was instituted only so as to strength-
en the intellect and preserve it from error—the necessity
for this arising out of the profound sciences, like physics
and metaphysics. As for the mathematical sciences, there is
no need in them for logic owing to their easiness and their
little entanglement with matter. Even if this were as they
say and logic were not necessary for the learning of the
10 mathematical sciences, their learning—if it came after
knowledge of it [sc., logic]—would undoubtedly be better.
And since we seek only the best in the study [to be done by]
this kind of humans, it is fitting that they begin with the
art of logic.

As for the nomos that it behooves them to accept during   ⌐
[this period of] study, why Plato—as was said before—   537
asserts of these that they are to be brought up on music.
When they reach sixteen or seventeen—and this is also after
they have rejected those dispositions [the rejection of which]
we have made a condition for them—they train in horse-
15 manship until they reach twenty. On reaching this, they go
on to the learning of philosophy, according to this [afore-
mentioned] order. Plato does not assert that they begin the
study of science prior to those years because their thought
is not yet settled nor have they perfected their ⌐cogitation⌐.   ⊢
Also, once the [contribution of] imitation to those stories on   539bc
which they grew up has been made clear to them, they

77.1-3   Compare 75.9, 11-12, above.

cannot be relied on not to ridicule them and proceed to
refute them before the multitude and to shatter them ⌜with⌝
20 objections. This is because their position, as Plato says, in
relation to the stories and speeches on which they were
raised is the position of one who grows up with whom he
takes to be his father and mother, coming to know when he
has grown strong and bestirred himself that he is a foundling
to the two of them and that his father and mother are others.
Do ⌜you⌝ not see that that earlier esteem of them would
pass away from his soul to the point that it sometimes would
lead him to mock them both? Similar is the case with this
25 kind of humans if they lay their hands on the sciences prior
to that age. This is because, in their zeal and ⌜sharpness⌝,
they will tear at the stories ⌜with argument⌝ just as a puppy
tears at the garment of whoever is close by. You will make
this clear [to yourself] for this happens frequently to the
pretenders to philosophy of these cities. This is the most
78. harmful of things in regard to them. | Thereafter they do
not cease reading science until they reach ⌜thirty⌝ and have
completed all its parts. When they reach thirty-five, they
are charged with the governance of the army; this is for
about fifteen years. When they are fifty years old they are
then fit for rulership in this city and to rule over it. When
they are too weak to do this on account of age, they return—
5 as Plato says—to the Isles of the Blessed. ⌜By the "Isles of
the Blessed" he means, according to what I think⌝, the
inquiry concerning the form [idea] of the good in whose
existence he believed. If there is someone who believes that
there is a good for man that exists for itself, he will believe

538a–
538c

540ab

78.1   thirty] Following Plato 539a and two MSS; other MSS: thirty-
five.

78.2   According to Plato 539e the guardians have to be forced to go
down again into the cave and compelled to take charge in the affairs
of war.

that the exercise of the other virtues hinders him from speculation on this. That is why, according to what I think, Plato asserts that at the end of their lives they isolate [themselves] for speculation ⌜upon⌝ that good.

10   He said: It is fitting for the citizens in general to mark off ⌐
certain days for them on which they recall their [sc., the rulers'] virtues; they bring offerings on [those days], offer sacrifices, and in general wax in praise of them in the manner that country folk do this. (The same is the case with the upbringing of women who are disposed by nature to lordship. We ⌜ourselves⌝ have already said that the woman shares in common with the man all the work of the
15   citizens.) Plato asserts that their governance of the city is fitting and proper if from them ⌜this⌝ city is provided with more than one man [to serve in their stead].

540b–
540e

When he finished this he resumed mentioning the manner by which to realize the possibility of the existence of this city in the best possible way. He had already said in what preceded that the emergence of this city is possible ⌜only if it happens⌝ that someone of this description among the wise is the son of a king or that rulership ⌜over these⌝ cities is fitting for him in other respects, such as excellence, numer-
20   ous relatives, honor, strength, and the rest. If this happens, ⊢
then the manner of the emergence of this city is this: He [sc., the qualified ruler] attends to those in his city who are more than ten years old or thereabouts; they expel them and send them to the villages; they take their children and bring them up in those disciplines and qualities that we have described. In this way the emergence of this city will
25   be quickest, easiest, and best. You ought ⌜to know⌝ that ⌞

541a

78.15   one man] or: one individual.
78.22   they] The shift in this sentence from the singular to the plural subject corresponds to what is left open in Plato 540d: when the true philosophers, either one or more, come to power in a city. . . .

this manner mentioned by Plato is the best for its emergence.

Its emergence is possible in a manner other than this, but [only] over a long time. This is when virtuous kings come to [rule] these cities in a succession—one after another and for a long time—not ceasing to incline these cities gradually until the situation in them, by the end of time, comes to be

79. the good governance. | Their [sc., these cities'] inclining will be of two kinds at once—i.e., in their actions and their deeds, and [in] their beliefs. This will be more or ⌜less⌝ easy, depending on the nomoi existing at any given time and on their [sc., the nomoi's] proximity to or distance from this city. In general, in this time their inclining to virtuous

5 deeds is more likely than their inclining to good beliefs. You can prove this from these cities. In general, one who has mastered the [several] parts of science and [understood] the manner of creating inclinations in them [sc., the cities] will have no difficulty in asserting that they are no better than the beliefs. The cities that are virtuous in deeds alone are those called aristocratic. It has been recounted that this city—i.e., the aristocratic—existed among the ancient Persians. These, then, are all the things Plato asserts con-

10 cerning the emergence of the virtuous city, its order, and the laying down of its nomoi. We have explained this with the utmost brevity possible for us. What yet remains for him

79.1-8   In a parallel passage in his paraphrase of Aristotle's *Rhetoric*, Averroes divides excellent dominion into (*a*) kingship, wherein both opinions and actions accord with what the theoretical sciences prescribe; and (*b*) the rule of the good, wherein only actions are virtuous. "This [latter governance] is known as the *imāmiyya*; it is said to have existed among the early Persians, according to Abū Naṣr [al-Fārābī]'s account" (Averroes, *Rhetoric*, 137.7-138.4) (Mahdi). See also Avempace, *Governance*, 11.4-5 (*MPP*, p. 128). The sharp distinction between beliefs and deeds drawn here by Averroes further emphasizes the contrast between the virtuous city and "these cities." "In this time" virtuous deeds are easier to come by than virtuous beliefs.

79.7, 8   aristocratic] *ha-mekaheneth* = *imāmiyya* (Mahdi).

of this part [of political science] is only what he says concerning the other unmixed, erring cities, how they may be
recognized, how this city may turn into them, and how they
turn into one another. As for the statement concerning the
manner in which these cities emerge, and setting up an
order for them whereby they may easily and in the best way
attain the utmost folly, which they leave for an inheritance:
15 why it seems that knowledge of this is not necessary for one
who possesses this science, just as it suffices for the physician
to know enough about ⌜poisons⌝ so as to recognize their
natures and know that it is proper to guard against them,
without troubling to learn the manner in which they are
made and compounded. So is it here with the philosopher
as regards these other cities—i.e., the erring cities. It suffices
him to recognize them and to know the evils that are
20 brought from them into the virtuous city. Hence what Plato
intended with this was to make known the manner in which
the virtuous city turns into them and they turn into one
another, and the comparison and contrast between them,
as well as what befalls them. We will cut off ⌜this⌝ treatise
here and begin the third treatise of this part [of political
science].

79.11, 26   unmixed] MSS: simple.
79.11, 18   erring cities] These cities are characterized as erring or
mistaken by Glaucon in 544a. "Erring cities" is also a technical term
as used by Farabi in *Political Regime*, 87.5, 104.3-6 (*MPP*, pp. 41 f., 53).
In Farabi's usage (followed by Averroes), the nonvirtuous cities to be
discussed in the third treatise are all "ignorant cities." See 52.22-23 and
note to 45.11, above.

The Third Treatise

Having completed the discussion in this part of this kind
[of governance], namely the discussion of the governance of
25 the virtuous cities, he turned to what remained for him of
this science, namely the discussion of nonvirtuous governances. He makes known only their unmixed kinds, and how
some turn into others, and the resemblance between them
and the virtuous governance and between one another. He
makes known which governance is most opposite ⌐to the
80. virtuous governance; and makes known | which may be set
down as being between these two governances—i.e., the
virtuous [and that] which is most opposite⌐ to it—being of
the rank of intermediaries between the extremes; and how
these intermediaries are arranged with respect to the extremes, as is the case with the other opposites that have more
than one intermediary between them and still are distinct.
5 An example of this is the color white. Black is its opposite.
Between the one and the other there are intermediaries;
these, however, are arranged—i.e., some are ⌐closer⌐ to
white and some are closer to black. It is evident that if this
is also the case with governance, the transformation of the
two extremes that are as opposite to each other as can be
will consist in their first turning into the intermediaries,

79.24-25   In admitting a plurality of virtuous cities, Averroes tacitly
rejects the notion of a single universal society based on the one true
religious Law. See 97.13, below, and 57.6 and note to 31.24-25, above.
For Farabi, too, there can be more than one virtuous city (*Political
Regime*, 102.3, 104.7 [*MPP*, pp. 51, 53]; *Plato*, 20.12 [Mahdi tr., p. 65];
Virtuous City, 70.9 [Dieterici tr., p. 111]).

and at that also according to the arrangement of the
intermediaries. That is, they first turn into the closest of
10 the intermediaries, then into that which follows it, later into
the one that follows it, ⌜until⌝ it turns into the extreme that
is most opposite [to it]. We shall explain this when we reach
Plato's words concerning this. Similarly we shall compare
the people who rule over each and every one of these
governances, in respect of themselves and of the pleasures
accruing to them from each and every governance and
⌜each and every guidance⌝.

15   This, then, is the sum of the necessary statements that
this part of Plato's statements comprehends. We ourselves
shall explain each and every thing that he says in it.

We say that Plato asserts that the unmixed governances
under which cities come into being are, in general, of five
kinds. The first kind is the virtuous governance, the discussion of which has preceded. The second is the primacy
of honor. The third is the primacy of the few, namely
20 rulership based on wealth; this is also known as the primacy
of the vile. The fourth is the primacy of the assembly of the
⌜multitude⌝. The fifth is the primacy of the tyrant. If you
divide the virtuous primacy into the primacy of the king
and the primacy of the good, then the primacies are six
[in number]. If someone takes charge of this governance in
whom five conditions are combined—namely wisdom, perfect understanding, good persuasion, good imagination, and
25 capability for war with no bodily impediment to his prac-

ticing martial acts—why he is the king simply and his governance is the truly royal governance. But if ⌜these⌝ qualities are only to be found separately in a group—so that one contributes to the end [of the city] through his wisdom, and the second [contributes] what leads to the end through his understanding, and the third has good persuasion in speech, and the fourth has good imagination, and

30 the fifth has capability for war—and they together help bring about and preserve this governance, why these are called select rulers and their rule is called the elevated and

81. choice rule. | It also may happen that the ruler of this city is one who has not attained this rank—i.e., the rank of king—but is expert in the nomoi that the first one [sc., the founder] legislated and has good [powers of] conjecture by which to extrapolate from them what the first one did not make clear for each and every decree and for each and every judgment. Of this class of knowledge is that knowl-

5 edge called by us the art of jurisprudence. Besides this he is to have a capability for war. This one is called a king [who rules] according to the laws. It may happen that these two are not found in a single individual, the warrior being other than the judge. The two of them must [then] necessarily share in lordship, as was the case with many of the Muslim kings. We hold that there is here yet ⌜another⌝ kind of governance. That is the governance of the pleasure-seeker;

assumes along with Rosenthal that the Hebrew translator mistook the meaning of *jihād*.

81.4 jurisprudence] The knowledge that is possessed by the second-rank ruler is *fiqh*. Averroes makes explicit what is implicit in the parallel passage in Farabi's *Aphorisms*. See also Farabi, *Enumeration*, 107.5-14 (*MPP*, p. 27), for the relative standing of jurisprudence; and Plato *Statesman* 301a–b.

81.6-7   Compare Farabi, *Virtuous City*, 61.7-9 (Dieterici tr., p. 97), where Farabi attributes wisdom to the one ruler and the remaining qualities to the co-ruler. Averroes' joint rulers appear to be below that rank.

10 that is the governance the end of whose citizens is pleasure
alone. If you join to this governance the necessity-govern-
ance, then the kinds of governance are eight. As for the
virtuous governance, the discussion of it has been completed.

As for the timocratic governance and the timocratic cities,
they are the cities that help their citizens to draw near to
15 honor and to attain it. Honor, in truth, is only between man
and man, when he thinks there is some perfection in the
other and subordinates his soul to him. There is here yet
another kind of honor performed without subordinating the
soul of the honorer to the honored. But here the honor is
balanced with another honor or money or advantage. This
honor consists only in equality, or else they are strict and
particular about equality as much as is possible—i.e., the
honor of the market-place.

As for the first kind of honor, it does not consist in
20 providing an abundance of things for which honor is obligatory. This kind of honor is that which is more fitting for
timocratic cities to aim at. Hence ranks are arranged in
them so that they resemble the virtuous city in this respect.
The difference between the two of them is that the honors
in the virtuous city are only something incidental to the
virtues and the fitting things that are truly fitting things, not
that the honor is intended for itself; rather it is a shadow
25 associated with the virtue. As for the timocratic cities, why
in them honor is intended for itself. It also is arranged by
them in accord with what is suitable—according to what
unexamined opinion holds to be suitable. These are among
the fitting things according to them: wealth, pedigree, whatever brings about the causes of pleasure, dice-playing, and
attaining most of the necessities; [also] since a man is able,

81.13 Averroes' account of timocracy, which continues to 82.20,
closely resembles Farabi's in *Political Regime*, 89.14-94.4 (*MPP*, pp. 43-
46). See also *Virtuous City*, 62.10-14 (Dieterici tr., p. 99).

through his wealth, to supply himself with all his needs, that
30 he be useful to others with respect to these things. It seems
that the things that ought to be most deserving of honor are
the love of violence and domination and that a man forever
be lord, not be lorded over, and be served, not serve. For
82. these | are already thought to be the primary virtue neces-
sarily leading to honor. And these are recognized among
humans as the great-souled, and especially when there is
joined to these the capability ⌜for⌝ victory and, in general,
for doing harm and for helping. The capability consists of
the improvement of the faculties of body and soul and of
5 the external means. Individuals of this description are those
who are lords in cities such as these. Their rank in honor
accords with their rank in these fitting things. Whoever is
not enabled by the honor from them to be a total lord, has
a partial lordship—lording it over in one respect and being
lorded over in another. Hence it is told of al-Manṣūr Ibn
Abī ʿĀmir that he used to go out to assemblages and
10 weddings and used to say: "Let whoever holds himself to be
prince of the faithful command me ⌜to humble myself⌝
before them. By my soul! I shall be honored by them, for he
does not honor the soul who does not humble and abase it."
In this governance they take precious garments for kings,
such as cloaks of byssus and purple, and seat [them] upon
golden thrones. For all these, according to unexamined
opinion, are [signs of] perfections and knowledge. The most
fitting of these for lordship is he through whom all these
desired things are assembled together and who is able to
15 allot them equitably among them and to preserve them.
This is the justice that exists in this city. It seems that this
city is the ⌜choicest⌝ of the nonvirtuous cities. This is because
it aims at the virtues that are virtues according to unexamined opinion and [at what], according to unexamined
opinion, are beautiful actions. Hence the likes of these seek

out actions by which a good memory may be left of them so
that they might be honored in their life and in their death.
This kind of association is the timocratic association. It is
20 rarely found in a simple nation; hence the existence of such
a city as this is difficult. But you yourself know that this
kind of governance ⌜was⌝ frequently found among us.

As for the governance of the vile, they are rulers whose
citizens care for wealth, riches, and the acquisition of this
in excess of need, not for the sake of ⌜receiving⌝ through
avarice anything for themselves other than them [sc., wealth
25 and riches]. Property is of two kinds: property by nature,
and property by convention. Natural property is what is
sought to supply the lack that befalls a man when he exists
without it. These are food, clothing, places wherein a man
may dwell or make room for himself by owning them, tools
that serve for these things, and materials out of which these
things [are made]. As for the property that is by convention,
83. that is dinars and dirhams and what | stands in their place.
These do not supply a natural lack in man and hence will
not be [found] in all cities. It is ⌜only⌝ the need for the
⌜provision of⌝ a medium [of exchange] that leads to them
in all activities in cities. Hence dinars and dirhams are an
appropriate sign for any money whatever if it happens to be
5 supplied by one who knows the conventional [equivalents].
⌜It is a sign⌝ of the proper [purchasing] power and the
initial appraisal of all things and a measure for them. This
is why it is thought to be identical with wealth and the most

82.22 Averroes' account, which continues to 83.15, elaborates upon
Farabi's discussion of the vile city in *Political Regime*, 88.14-89.6 (*MPP*,
p. 43). See also *Virtuous City*, 62.6-8 (Dieterici tr., p. 98).

83.2 all cities] See 43.13-31, above.

83.2-3 medium of exchange] *v'ūlam ha-ṣōrekh ha-mēbhi' ēlēyhem
bemedīnōth bekhal ha-maʿaśīm ⟨v⟩ēṣel hōṣa'ath ha-emṣaʿī*. Perhaps, following
other MSS: leads to them in acquisitive [or: democratic] cities.

83.4 supplied] MSS: loved.

fitting of things to be accumulated and acquired. That is
because it is potentially all things valuable, besides being
easily transferable. The ruler of these [people] is the
wealthiest and most powerful among them. If, joined to
this, he has the capability of governing them well in that he
acquires wealth for them and preserves it for them always,
10 why then he is suitable for being the lord over this city.
Wealth is obtained first from all the necessary things, such
as agriculture, grazing, and hunting; later on, from trading,
hiring, and the rest. This is the association based on wealth
and the purpose that this association has in view. This
lordship is known as the lordship of the few because in their
15 seeking to acquire ⌜property⌝ it necessarily follows that
they will be few and that the majority in this city be the
poor, as will appear later on.

As for the democratic association, it is the association in
which everyone in it is unrestrained. He does what his heart
desires and moves toward whichever of the pleasing things
his soul leads him. Hence there will emerge in this city the
totality of things that exist separately in those [other] cities.
20 So there will be among them people who are lovers of honor,
and humans who love the possession of property, and
humans who love tyranny. Nor is it farfetched that there be
among them one who has the virtues and is moved by them.
Hence all the arts and ⌜dispositions⌝ emerge in this city,
and it is so disposed that from it may emerge the virtuous
city and every one of the other cities. It seems that there is
no lordship here other than by the will of those who accept
25 being lorded over on account of the primary laws. For it is

83.8-12 Compare the parallel passage in Farabi, *Political Regime*,
89.4-6 (*MPP*, p. 43). "Necessary things" corresponds to Farabi's
"methods employed to obtain the bare necessities." Averroes here omits
the fourth in Farabi's enumeration: robbery.

83.16 On democracy see Farabi, *Political Regime*, 99.7-101.5 (*MPP*,
pp. 50 f.); and *Virtuous City*, 62.16-18 (Dieterici tr., p. 99).

also thought concerning this city that it is not fitting that
all things be permitted every man in it, for thereby it would
come to their killing and ⌜robbing⌝ one another, since this
too is one of the desires fixed in the nature of many humans.
Hence there is no doubt that the primary laws are observed
by people, namely [those regulating] the sites chosen by the
citizens on their first coming to that city and also the food

84. found | there. After that there are the secondary laws
concerning commerce, and similarly also tertiary laws concerning [moral] dispositions and what resembles them. It is
evident that in this city the household is the primary
intention and the city is only for its sake. Hence it is entirely
domestic, contrary to what is ⌜the case with⌝ the virtuous

5 city. Every man, if he so wills, may have all goods in
private. If so, most of these cities existing today are democratic, and the individual who truly lords it over them is the
one who has the capability of so governing that every man
attains his desire and preserves it. This city is the one of
which most of the multitude hold that it is the city to be
admired, for every man asserts on the basis of unexamined

10 opinion that he deserves to be free. It seems that this city
is the first among the cities that grow out of the necessity-
cities; for once humans attain the necessary, they are
aroused toward their desires, and this city [sc., the democratic city, then] necessarily comes into being. The association in these cities is necessarily only accidentally an
association since ⌜they do not aim at⌝ a single end in their
association, and the lordship in them is lordship ⌜only⌝ by

84.3-4 Avempace, *Governance*, 6.2-6 (*MPP*, pp. 124 f.).

84.10 the necessity-cities] or: the indispensable cities. See Farabi,
Political Regime, 88.4-13 (*MPP*, pp. 42 f.); and *Virtuous City*, 62.4-6
(Dieterici tr., p. 98). See 86.24-27, below.

84.12 do not aim at] MS *A*: since it is impossible [to have].

84.12-15 See note to 52.25-26, above.

chance. The associations of many of the Muslim kings today
15 are only associations that are entirely domestic. All that
remains in them of the nomos is the nomos that preserves
the primary laws for them. It is evident that all property in
this city is domestic. Hence they ⌜sometimes⌝ need to bring
forth ⌜from the household⌝ some of the acquired surplus in
it and transfer it to whichever of them fights. Herein
originate tributes and imposts. Men are of two classes: a
class designated the multitude, and a class designated the
20 mighty—as was the case with the people in ⌜Persia⌝ and as
is the case in many of these cities of ours. Among these the
multitude are plundered by the mighty, and the mighty go
so far in seizing their property that this occasionally leads
them to tyranny, just as this comes about in this time of ours
and in this city of ours. For the most part, love of property
grows upon the multitude only when the primary nomoi
among them are acquisitive. When every one fights for the
25 city, he is not obliged to draw off any of his wealth for
fighting. This will occur ⌜only⌝ as long as humans hold fast
to that which was laid down for them—the nomos of the
citizens of the necessity-cities—and especially if their liveli-
hoods depend on hunting or robbery. But when different
desires arise in them and grow to extremes, it is impossible
for them as a whole to fight and their kings need to impose
30 ⌜taxes⌝ upon them. If, along with this, it should happen that
these rulers do not equitably divide the property seized
85. from them | and lord it over them, why this is the hardest of
things for the multitude. They will then try to shake off
the rulers, and the lord will try to tyrannize over them.
Hence this city is most opposite to the tyrannical city. What

84.13   by chance] Farabi, *Political Regime*, 101.9-10 (*MPP*, p. 51):
for here no one has a better claim than anyone else to a position of
authority.

84.19   mighty] *taqīfīm*. See note to 41.17, above.

84.20   Persia] Plato *Laws* 3. 697c–698a.

initially was designated as civic property in this nation is by
now truly domestic—i.e., for the sake of the households of
5 the lords among them. Hence the aristocratic part among
them is by now entirely tyrannical. This, then, is the
situation of the democratic city and the matters related to it.

As for the truly tyrannical cities, they are the cities
through the association and efforts of whose citizens the
completion of a single aim is intended, namely the aim of
the tyrant to attain the end he has set for himself. This may
be only the desire for tyrannizing, or the desire for honor,
10 or the desire for wealth, or ⌐the desire for⌐ pleasure, or the
combination of them. It is evident that the likes of these
[things] are not sought for any end for which they are
intended other than serving the tyrant and giving
expression to his will. Hence they resemble slaves; indeed
they are truly slaves. This association is the most opposite
to the virtuous association ⌐because in the virtuous association it is intended only that every one of the citizens
receive as much of happiness as it is in his nature to be
15 raised to. Hence the intention of the virtuous royal arts⌐ is
only the advantage of the civic body, just as is the case with
the other arts. An example of this is the art of medicine: its
intention is the healing of the sick, not the attainment of

85.5   aristocratic] *kohanī* = *imāmī.* See note to 79.1-8, above.

85.7   tyrannical cities] or: despotic cities. See Farabi, *Political Regime,*
94.5-99.6 (*MPP,* pp. 46-50); and *Virtuous City,* 62.14-16 (Dieterici tr.,
p. 99).

85.12-14   Farabi defines political science as the knowledge of the
things by which the citizens may thus attain happiness (*Attainment,*
16.4-5 [*MPP,* p. 61]). That Averroes should then go on, as he does in
the next sentence, to speak of virtuous royal arts is not surprising in the
light of Plato *Statesman* 259a–b, 305c–e, and Aristotle *Nicomachean Ethics*
1. 2. 1094a26–b10.

85.15   civic body] The reference is to those people who participate
in the affairs of the city, political humans, as distinguished from gods
and subpolitical beings.

85.15-18   Plato 342d–e, 346e.

the physician's private intention. Similarly, the navigator's
intention is the saving of the ship's crew, not the saving of
himself alone—as is the case with the tyrant's intention. For
he aims at his own private intention. He does not grant them
20 any advancement, but ⌐only⌐ grants them necessary things
to the extent that they serve him utterly, as is done with
slaves. It is evident that this city is of the utmost injustice
since not one of the practical arts has as its intention solely
the completion of the intention of the arts. This is self-
evident. The governance of the household of the citizens of
this city and the other arts and crafts existing in it aim
25 solely at the perfection of a single intention and solely at
the life of a single household, without anyone having an
intention of his own. So also with the virtuous city: the
households and other kinds of people in it also only aim, in
their intention, ⌐at⌐ the good of one [kind] of people, namely
the lords, who in this respect resemble the tyrannical city.
But the difference between them is this: notwithstanding
30 that the other kinds of people in each of these two [cities]
aim only at the completion of a single intention alone, in
the virtuous city this is only so that every one of its kinds
may have an intention sought by it for itself, in that this is
86. its happiness. | When it is added that this intention is for
the sake of those who are kings over them, then the intentions of the citizens are for the sake of their [sc., the lords']
intentions. Hence each one of the two kinds—i.e., that of
the lord and that of the multitude—helps its fellow in the
virtuous city attain happiness. That is, the multitude serve
the lords in that whereby the intention of wisdom is fulfilled
in them [sc., the lords]; and the lords serve the multitude in
5 that which brings them to their happiness—if such as this
can be called service. It would be more proper that it be
be called governance or guidance. Such is not the case in
the tyrannical city, for in it and as regards the multitude,

the lords seek no intention other than their private intention. Therein is the similarity between aristocratic cities and tyrannical cities. The aristocratic parts existing in these
10 cities ⌈often⌉ turn into tyrannical ones, and give the lie to the aristocratic intention—as is the case with the aristocratic parts found in cities existing in this time of ours. The tyrant necessarily has helpers among them, and consequently tyrannizes over the citizens. It may, however, happen that these helpers and mighty ones are not accorded advancement by tyrannical lordship; this city is tyrannical in its entirety. It may indeed happen that they have some
15 superiority from tyrannical lordship, their varying [status] in this lordship corresponding to the extremity of their tyranny and their violence. This kind of tyranny exists most frequently, particularly at the beginning of a tyranny. This city tyrannizes over its kind—I mean that the mighty in it, together with the king, tyrannize over the multitude. Indeed, it may happen that the citizens as a whole help to tyrannize the other nations, not to tyrannize one another. Their rank would then correspond to their rank in capa-
20 bility for tyrannizing and in the soundness of their plans for saving and preserving them[selves]. Their first lord will be whichever of them is most advanced in these things. These, then, are the tyrannical cities and their kinds.

As for the cities based on pleasure, they are the ones whose citizens, through their association, aim at the attainment of sensual pleasure such as eating, drinking, copu-

---

86.8-10   aristocratic] *kohanī* = *imāmī*. See note to 79.1-8, above. See also Averroes' discussion (63.27-64.22) of the deleterious effects of these cities upon virtuous natures and the political consequences of the deterioration of those individuals.

86.15   varying] or: manifold.

86.22   Farabi's "base city." See *Political Regime*, 89.7-13, 102.12-103.13 (*MPP*, pp. 43, 52 f.); and *Virtuous City*, 62.8-10 (Dieterici tr., pp. 98 f.).

lation, and the others. Similarly the necessity-cities are
those whose citizens, through their association, aim at the
25 attainment of the necessary things. That through which they
attain the necessary things are either agriculture or hunting
or robbery. Agriculture is of them all [the most] natural to
man for the attainment of the necessary. This much of a
notion of these cities as is here [presented] will suffice
according to the intention of this science in its primary
purpose. These governances are varied and many in accord
30 with the varying states of the soul. Hence they must necessarily ⌈point⌉ to the states of the soul; and the cause of their
being of this number is nothing other than that [this is] the
87. number of the states of the soul. | The spirited part is that
which loves honor; when it goes too far it becomes tyrannical. As for the love of pleasure and wealth, this necessarily
belongs to the desiring part. As for the democratic city and
the cause of its coming into being, why it is the variety in
the states of the soul and the appetite that is fixed in the
nature of each and every man with regard to each and
5 every one of these states. If the parts of the soul are severed
from one another and the baser of them is not for the sake
of the nobler—as many humans may possibly assert—then
the human association is the association of the free. Similarly, if the parts of the soul are for the sake of the spirited
part, then the human association is the timocratic or
tyrannical association. Hence, too, if the desiring soul is the
leading one, then the association based on wealth or the
10 hedonistic one is the virtuous association. It has already
been made clear in physics and in this science ⌈as well that
the case is quite the opposite of all this and⌉ that the
lordship over the parts of the soul belongs only to the

86.24-27   See 83.10-12 and note to 84.10, above.
87.11   rational part] Plato 586e; Aristotle *Nicomachean Ethics* 10. 7.
1177a12-18.

rational part. Hence the virtuous city is the city over which
this part rules.

This having been made clear concerning the ends of these
cities, it is fitting that we proceed to each and every thing
that Plato says about the transformation of these cities into
15 one another and the comparison between them. He first
begins by comparing these cities in pairs, thereafter comparing the two people who rule over the two of them.
Finally he compares them all together, since the case is
clearer in governances than it is in states [of the soul]. Just
as justice is clearer in a city than it is in the ⌐particular⌐
soul, so it appears to be with wrongdoing. We resume and
20 we say: Although this city—i.e., the virtuous one—once it ⌐
exists, ⌐does not easily⌐ perish, it undoubtedly does perish 546
necessarily since everything that comes into being perishes,
as has been explained in physics and becomes clear through
investigation. As to whence corruption enters into it, why
it is clear that it enters into it from the class that rules over
it when there arise in it [sc., the ruling class] confusion,
corruption, and the mixture of the golden and silver
[classes]. So that when the lords in this city do not attend
25 to the selection of like [individuals] for copulation in the
manner that he said, there are born to them children who
do not resemble ⌐them⌐. If these are not transferred from
the class of guardians but remain guardians, the bad ones
among them will constantly shun those things on which
they have been raised and despise music and choose gymnastic, [thereby] strengthening the spirited part in them and
the desiring part. When this kind of humans arises in the ⊢
class of lords and is mixed with the virtuous kind, then each 547
one of them pulls his fellow to what resembles him. The
30 bronze and iron kind will be zealous to acquire and possess

87.21   physics] Aristotle *Physics* 5. 2. 226a6-8.
87.30   Or: to acquire property and be master over them.

property, while the other kind will be zealous for those
88. primary virtues. | If the pulling between them is prolonged,
they settle on something intermediate between the virtuous
governance and the governance in which property is accumulated. They [sc., the bronze and iron kinds who are now
part of the guardian class] take possession of land, houses,
and chattels for themselves in particular. They give the
[gold and silver] guardians as much of this as is needed to
sustain them, turning them by this act from free friends
into slaves who are lorded over because of their [sc., the
5   bronze and iron rulers'] might in war and their love of
training and honor. It is evident that this governance is like
something in the middle between the governance based on
wealth, namely the lordship of the few, and the virtuous
lordship. For in the respect in which this class among them
that fights for them does not wish anything of the acquisition of property or of the other arts, it resembles the
virtuous city. But in the respect that the lords in it are not
those virtuous ones whom we have defined—those tending
10 toward lordship being rather those who are spirited and
have a capability for victory—it is likewise not virtuous. ⊢
Hence this governance is a mixture of good and bad. Now ⁵⁴⁸ᶜ
this lordship is the first lordship that Plato ⌜asserts⌝ the
virtuous city is transformed into because preference for
honor, violence, and love of lording-it-over prevail over the
souls of the virtuous more than the other desires. That is
why those who are skilled in debate say that [what begins
15 as] the lordship of friends ends up as the love of honor.
Furthermore, this is the first thing to be chosen after
wisdom, according to unexamined opinion, since honor is
a shadow that accompanies it. It is, as it were, the closest
thing into which the virtuous are transformed. It is not

88.14-15   One sees dimly here a play on words in the original: what
begins as the lordship of lovers ends up as the love of lordship.

often that there are to be found those who are free of it
[sc., love of honor] because of prolonged [association] with
it and love of being remembered. If one's love of honor goes
to the point of tyrannizing, then he withdraws himself from
such cities as these, which have the virtuous kind of lordship,
20 no less [surely] than if the bad class accept the lordship of
a tyrant or if one of this description grows up among them.
This, then, is what Plato asserts concerning the initial
transformation of the virtuous governance. He holds similarly concerning the transformation of the individual who
resembles the virtuous governance, namely the philosopher,
into the individual who resembles the timocratic association, namely he whose happiness consists in honor.

He said and characterized this individual—he means the
one whose happiness consists in honor—as being an indi-
25 vidual who prefers gymnastic, loves hunting, rejects music,
loves lordship and tyranny, and does not base his claim to
lordship on what he says or suggests but rather on his
strength in war.

548d–
549e

He said: He who is of this character will undoubtedly
despise money as long as he is a youth, but as he grows
older there is born ⌜in him⌝ with the passing days a love
of money. ⌜This is because⌝ his nature is not a complete
nature. In the end, he participates in the money-lover's
nature since he already has been abandoned by the best
30 guardian to the extent that he removes himself from
89. listening to the musical arguments. If the soul bends | to
them [sc., the musical arguments] from its beginning, it
persists all its life in preferring virtue. This, then, is the
character of the individual whose happiness consists in
honor. But how does this individual grow out of the virtuous one? This will be when this young fellow happens to be
the son of a virtuous individual who grew up in a city
5 without a good governance. He [sc., the father] flees from

the honors and lordships established therein and from
whoever in general conducts it at some level. He removes
himself from all things, as happens to the virtuous who
come forth in nonvirtuous cities. This being so, and this
being the situation of the father of this young fellow, the
first thing that happens to him is that he hears from his
mother that she is discontented with her husband—i.e., his
parent—because ⌐he is not one of the lords; because of this
she lacks standing among its citizens; moreover, she has a
10 hard life because⌐ he also does not wish to accumulate
wealth or to seek it. Hence she repeatedly tells her son,
"You have a father who has not the nature of a man and is
very lax," and the rest of what women customarily censure
men with. The same holds for the servant of this young
fellow and his friend and in general whoever gives heed to
his bidding from among the inhabitants of his household.
When [one of the latter] sees the parent of this one set upon
by ⌐someone⌐ who oppresses him or hits him, he commands
15 [that individual's] son (while he is yet a young fellow) to
take revenge on whoever oppressed his father and inflict
twice as much of the oppression upon him [when he grows
up]; and in general, in all his actions, to be more like a
man ⌐in his appearance and in⌐ his courage than his parent.
This being so, there is ⌐further⌐ joined to him in this city ⊢—
the opinion of its citizens calling one who minds his own   550ab
business a fool and a madman and a defective and a
simpleton, while those who attend to those who are not of
their way of life and meddle into what are not their affairs
20 are honored and praised and called mighty. In such a lad,
the virtuous nature that his father nurtured in him, namely
the cogitative soul, draws him on together with the desiring
and spirited nature that ⌐these⌐ [people] do not cease

89.15   Following Plato 549e.

nurturing in him. From this he turns to something intermediate between excess love of the desires and love of
virtue. He thrusts the lordship in himself to the middle part,
namely love of honor, since this part of the soul, as we have ⌊
said repeatedly, is of all the parts that which is closest to the
25 part leading to virtue. He necessarily turns into an individual who loves honor ⌜and acts haughtily⌝. This, then,
is the character of the youth who is among those whose
happiness consists in honor, and the character of his transformation from the virtuous nature. He resembles the
character of the timocratic city and its transformation from
the virtuous city. You may understand what Plato says
concerning the transformation of the virtuous governance
into the timocratic governance and of the virtuous individual into the timocratic individual from the case of the
30 governance of the Arabs in early times, for they used to
imitate the virtuous governance. Then they were transformed into timocrats in the days of Muʿāwiya. So seems
to be the case in the governance now existing in these
islands.

After this he investigates which governance this timo-
90. cratic city might possibly be transformed into | and into
which of the other people who rule over cities this timocratic
individual ⌜might possibly⌝ be transformed. He says that
this governance—i.e., the timocratic—is for the most part ⌈

89.28-31 Averroes points to two latter-day cases that come close to
illustrating Plato's account of the transformation of the virtuous governance. The first concerns the regime of the Arabs under Muhammad
and his immediate successors, the first four caliphs (632-661), here
described as an "imitation" of the virtuous governance. In the accession
of the caliph Muʿāwiya in 661 and the establishment of the Umayyad
dynasty, Averroes sees a transformation of the imitation. The second
case refers to the Almohad dynasty, under whose rule of Morocco and
Andalus Averroes lived the greater part of his life. See 92.4-8, below.
  89.32 Paragraphing supplied.
  90.4 See 82.22-83.15, above.

transformed into the lordship of the few. This lordship, as
5 we have said, is lordship of the rich; the poor have no share
whatever in lordship among them. The transformation of
the timocratic into this governance occurs only because,
over time, they come to see the utility in dinars and dirhams
and prefer the useful to the beautiful. They withdraw from
virtue by another evil stage within the timocratic city ⌐and
accord dinars and dirhams a shameful honor. It is possible ∟
to observe that which Plato speaks of when we investigate
10 the timocratic cities⌐ and how they are transformed. This
lordship is a vile, despicable, and contemptible lordship; it
is of little stability, perishing through some little thing that
comes upon it from without or within. The first error in it ⌐
is that they do not award lordship to him who has the ⁵⁵¹
capacity to maintain it. Rather they only look out that he
be sufficiently wealthy alone. In this they are in the position
of one who chooses that the pilot of the ship be whoever
15 among the ship's company is most avaricious; and they do
not heed the captain who is truly a captain ⌐regarding the
rule of the ship, on account of his being poor⌐. Whoever
does this has already undoubtedly prepared the ship for
destruction. So is the case with the city. Further, this city
is not a single city, but rather two cities—the city of the
poor and the city of the rich. For if they accumulate
property and are niggardly with it, they will remain non-
20 poor. An evil affecting this city is that they are [rendered]
utterly incapable for war because the situation compels
them to [adopt] one of two [courses]. [*a*] They may employ
many fighters, but ⌐this⌐ is impossible for them because of
fear of them. (Hence he says of their lordship that it is the
lordship of the few.) Also, they are stingy with their
property, so in this respect too it is impossible for them to

90.15   ship] MSS: city.

employ many mighty ones. [*b*] If they themselves are the
25 fighters or some few of them, then when they wage war they
will flee. You can make this clear from the case of most
easeful nations when poor nations make war with them. Of
necessity there must be an error in this lordship of the sort
he did not leave off censuring in what preceded, [namely]
that one is occupied with many things, such as farming and
accumulating wealth.   ⊢

He said: The generation of this kind of lords in this ⁵⁵²
30 governance is the greatest of the evils that come upon them.
That is because they never cease turning the governance
toward whatever is advantageous for them, particularly in
the acquisition of wealth. Undoubtedly it will be one of the
91. nomoi laid down in this city | that it is not proper that
aristocrats rule over them or theirs, and that every man may
give away all his wealth, and nomoi similar to these. This
5 being so, the poor in this city increase of necessity just as
increase the drones born in a beehive who eat but do not
gather honey. Just as the drones are the greatest disease for
the beehive, so is the case in this city. This being so, where
there are poor in the city so are there necessarily robbers,
plunderers, and bad people. Hence such cities as these have
10 in them many kinds of evil. This, then, is the wrongdoing ⌐
and the error that beset this city. For the most part, the
timocratic city is devoid of this; hence that city is closer to
the virtuous city, and the distance of this [sc., the oligarchic
city] from it is proportionate to the error that befalls it.

After having made clear how the timocratic city is trans-

90.30-91.2 Averroes' addition to, or substitution for, Plato 552a–b.
91.3-4 increase of necessity] Other MSS add: and remain as thorns
and pricks in the eyes of the rich, who are few in number. Such plagues
as these in this city resemble the drones. . . . (The phrase "thorns and
pricks in the eyes" combines expressions found in Num. 33:55 and
Josh. 23:13.)
91.13 Paragraphing supplied.

formed into this city, and how many kinds of error befall
it, and what kind of governance it has, it is proper that we
15 also consider the individual who resembles it, in which city
he is and out of what he is transformed. We say: When the
one for whom happiness consists in honor has a son and 553
successor, it may possibly happen later on that he ⌐grows
poor⌐ and that everything that he owned passes away.
Moreover, he is drawn toward some one of the lordships,
such as governance of the army and the like, and there are
lawsuits against him owing to people who ⌐bring him up⌐
to judgment and render him contemptible. When some-
20 thing like this or resembling it happens to him, dying will
be more bearable for him than the poverty that has beset
him. Love of honor is expelled from the soul of whoever
prefers the acquisition of wealth, and for this he sends forth
all the desires. Such is the transformation of the timocratic
individual into the oligarchic one. He undoubtedly resembles the governance based on wealth, just as the individual
whom we characterized as being one whose happiness
consists in honor also resembles that [timocratic] govern-
25 ance. This individual undoubtedly is avaricious and
niggardly; he finds it sufficient that civic desires are [limited 554a,
to] the necessary things, but he does not do this out of any 554e
virtue in him. He only abandons these desires for another
desire that is greater in him, namely the love of wealth.
Hence, if the likes of these are denied others' property ⌐but⌐
do not refrain from unnecessary desires, there will be rapid
ruin and destruction, as we have said, on account of the
30 niggardliness in them. In general, the transformation of the
timocratic individual into the hedonistic individual is something evident, whether he takes his pleasure in wealth or
92. the other remaining pleasures. So seems | to be the case with

91.22   oligarchic] Literally: moneyed.
91.28   them] MSS: him.

the timocratic city and the hedonistic city; this is because
the ⌜city⌝ based on wealth and the hedonistic one are of a
single class. We often see kings being corrupted ⌜to⌝ the
likes of these. An example in this time is the kingdom of
5 people known as the Almoravids. At first they imitated the
governance based on the nomos; this was under the first
one of them. ⌜Then they changed under his son into the
timocratic, though there also was mixed in him the love of
wealth⌝. Then it changed under his grandson into the
hedonistic with all the kinds of things of the hedonists; and
it perished in his days. This was because the governance
that opposed it at that time resembled the governance based
on the nomos. This, then, is the statement on the change
of the timocratic individual into the oligarchic individual.
10 The difference between their two ranks is clear, for the
oligarchic is baser than the timocratic. So is the case with
the city of them both. Now we ought to consider into which
city this city can possibly be changed out of itself.

We say that he says that it changes into the democratic ⌈
city. Similarly, he also explains further that the oligarchic   555b–
individual changes into the individual resembling this city.   555d

92.1-2 See 81.9-10, above.

92.4 Almoravids] Correcting the Hebrew mistranslation. The
Almoravids were the dynasty that preceded the Almohads (see note to
89.28-31, above).

92.4-8 What began as an "imitation" of the governance based on
the nomos under the conqueror Yūsuf Ibn Tāshfīn (1061-1107) was
twice transformed by the time his grandson reigned forty years later.
The latter's overthrow was effected by ʿAbd al-Muʾmin, the founder of
the Almohad dynasty, whose governance "at that time resembled" the
governance based on the nomos. In the absence of further evidence,
the governance based on the nomos cannot simply be equated with the
governance based on the Law. Averroes would have had no difficulty
whatever in expressing that if such had been his intention. The model
for the imitation or resemblance, the standard by which these regimes
are being judged, is not the Koran, but rather that which the Koran
itself incorporates and imitates. See note to 62.29-63.1, above.

15 As for the mode by which the city based on wealth is changed into this city, it is this: Since lordship in the city of the few is assured only by the possession of property alone, their nomoi that they lay down necessarily [include] a nomos that helps them in this intention. Hence the first thing they lay down as a principle of the nomos is that it be permitted any one of the youths who so wishes to spend whatever he wishes of his wealth on whatever desire he wishes. For thereby it comes about that they [sc., the money-
20 grubbers] draw off all their wealth. This is why it is impossible for people in this lordship to combine with the honoring of wealth and its acquisition, the laying-down of nomoi regarding moderation, [even] when because of necessity they have to propose them and especially at the end when they lay down nomoi such as these. When they forsake people and their desires, they forsake not a few to go to poverty, but many—and these not only the undistinguished, but [also] those of nobility and courage.
25 When such as these come forth in this city and multiply in it, they necessarily anger the avaricious and niggardly, whom they envy and blame for being the cause that placed them in poverty and contempt. Similarly, they lay down many nomoi in this city.

      ⊢
      556b–
      556e

    He said: They make their souls idle and put them at ease since they do not attend to things other than the accumulation of wealth.

    He said: When many people of this kind of poverty are
30 associated together and there come forth among them such drones ⌈as are born⌉ in beehives, and they compare themselves with the rich in battles and in the other civic affairs that are imposed upon them by the necessity of association,
93. they find themselves | mightier than they in everything. And they despise them and assert that they became wealthy only because of their [sc., the poor's] shame and disgrace.

The situation of this city is then like the ⌜situation⌝ of a shattered and sickly body. Just as a body of this character falls ill from the slightest external cause, so is the case with this city. If there is some city opposing it—and particularly
5 a democratic one—then such drones as these who come forth, help them against them [sc., the rich] and agree to plunder the rich and seize their wealth and drive them from the city or enslave them. Just as it is also possible for a body to take leave of its own being and change, so is it possible that this city change from its being into the democratic city. This comes about when the poor that are in it conspire against the rich and ransack their property and kill them
10 or drive them from the city. You can explain this by [referring to] the niggardliness and avarice [displayed] toward the poor in these cities on [the part of] the rich. When this is so and the likes of these—the free-born poor— rule over the city, every one of them does what is right in his eyes. Lordship among them is held by some kind of chance. Every kind of human is undoubtedly to be found in this city, and no ⌜one⌝ has any rank at all. Their nomos is an equal nomos—i.e., there is no superior among them.
15 Hence this city—i.e., the democratic one—resembles a many-colored woven garment. Just as this kind of garment is considered by women and youths to be good because of the variety of its colors, so seems to be the thought about this city according to unexamined opinion. But in truth it is not so. Unless strengthened by virtue or honor, it perishes rapidly, as is the case with democratic cities existing in this
20 time of ours and in that which preceded [it]. Out of this city will come forth the virtuous city and the other kinds of these cities because they exist in it potentially since all the

557a–
557c

93.12-13 chance] I.e., lordship is not attained because of some particular merit. See 84.13, above, and note thereto. See also Averroes, *Rhetoric*, 136.11-12.

states of the soul exist in ⌜this city⌝. So it seems that the first cities to grow up by nature are the necessity-cities; then the democratic cities follow them; then every one of these cities branches off from them. Hence, as Plato says, the wise ought to attend to such cities as these [sc., the democratic ones]
25 and choose from among them the good kinds that accord with the virtuous association ⌜until⌝ they bring it forth. This is analogous to a man who wishes to set up a store in ⌜ which he sells everything and who chooses from it that 557/de which pleases him.

He said: Since in this city no one is compelled to undertake any of the ⌜useful⌝ civic matters ⌜such as⌝ wars, peace, and the rest, it easily comes to ruin. Hence it is that we see ⊢ people such as these who deserve being put to death 558
30 dwelling among them as though [no one cared or saw, stalking the land like a hero].

He said: Moreover, they do not praise the things that we ourselves were praising when we were attending to ⌜the virtuous city⌝, nor do they adhere to any of those actions. |
94. This, then, is the extent of the error in this city and its remoteness from the virtuous city, even though it might be thought of this governance, according to unexamined opinion, that it is a hedonistic governance. This, then, is the statement concerning the transformation of the city based on wealth into the democratic one, and the extent of the error that befalls it in comparison to the virtuous city and the timocratic city.

5   We ought also to consider the individual resembling it and out of what he changes. We say that the individual who

93.21-23 Averroes' addition.

93.30 Following Plato 558a. MSS have instead a near-quotation from Isa. 43:10: they are those before whom there was no God formed.

94.1-4 Averroes' summary.

94.5 Paragraphing supplied.

resembles this lordship also only changes from being a
citizen of the lordship of the few in the [same] manner as
this city changes from it [sc., the oligarchic city]. It may
happen that a son is born to that individual who is a citizen
of the lordship of the few, and, for want of education in the
lordship of the few and because of the increase of idlers that
come forth there, he does not leave off bending his son
10 toward his governance. [Meanwhile] those without bend
him [sc., the son] toward absolute freedom and aim at this
kind of desires. As time passes he necessarily changes to
unqualified freedom in all his desires, not limiting [himself]
to the necessary desires with which his father would have
him be satisfied. Rather he will move to the unnecessary
desires. (By "necessary desires" I mean those that are ⌊
constituted in us and which we need for life, such as the
desire for water and food with respect to this preserving the
15 humors of our bodies ⌜by transmitting to our bodies⌝ a
replacement for that which pours out of ⌜them⌝.) Now if ⌈
this youth turns to some such condition, he will from day ⁵⁶¹
to day become more subjected to his desires that come into
his mind. At one time he drinks wine till he is drunk; at
another time he drinks water till his temperament cools; at
another time he takes gymnastic with those who engage in
gymnastic; at another time his conduct is like the conduct
of those who engage in philosophy; and at other times he is
20 slothful and too relaxed for any activity. In general, there
is neither order nor measure in his conduct. Yet this conduct is called sweet and free, though in truth it is the
remotest of things from human conduct. For inasmuch as
man has some single end, his activity necessarily only
[corresponds] to some single governance. This youth being ⌊
then of this disposition, he necessarily resembles the democratic city. We presuppose that this is so and that the
comparison between him and these people whom we have

25 enumerated is like the comparison between the cities. We ought to consider which city this city—i.e., the democratic one—changes into and what is its potentiality, and into which individual this individual turns, and what is his rank and measure and happiness.

He said that the democratic cities mostly change into ⌐
30 tyranny and the tyrannical cities. The case of the change 562ab of the democratic city into the tyrannical one is like the case of the change of the lordship of the few into the democratic lordship. The cause of this is of one class: for just as the cause of the change of the lordship of the few into the
95. democratic lordship is nothing | other than excess in the end that they aim at, namely the acquisition of wealth (for this is the cause of so many democratic people coming forth in that city, they being those whom we likened to drones ∟ existing in beehives), so the cause of the change of demo-cratic lordship into the tyrannical lordship is only excess in ⌐
5 quest of freedom and the limitless ⌐increase⌐ of it. For 563e–564d whatever is done in excess goes beyond its measure and is changed into the opposite. This occurs not only in voluntary things but also in natural things. The quest for excess in ⌐freedom⌐ is the cause of there coming forth in it drones ⌐resembling⌐ the drones that come forth in the lordship of the few, save that here it [sc., the cause] is more extensive
10 and more frequent. That is because the lords in that city— i.e., the city of the few—do not praise such as these who come forth among them—i.e., idlers full of desires—but rather destroy and fight them. Hence its change is to ∟ something intermediate between the city based on wealth and the tyrannical city, and this is the democratic city. Such men as these as come forth among them are the ⌐ honored and praised ones whom they set up as lords for 562d–563d
15 them, and [these] rule ⌐over⌐ them. For it is the way of this lordship that when freedom overflows in it they are stirred

up in their households and dwellings and in all the classes
to be found among them to the point that fathers and sons,
masters and slaves, men and women, are placed on an equal
footing among them. And they nullify the law in order that
nothing have lordship over them. In general, nothing is
choiceworthy among them save absolute freedom and that
a man control whatever he wants as he wants. Of necessity, ⊢—
20 then, the coming-forth of that bad class of drones will   564b–
increase among them just as ⌈the production of humors⌉   564e
increases in shattered bodies—⌈i.e.,⌉ phlegm, and the red
and the black [bile]—to the point that this city, with such
a class as this coming forth in it, turns necessarily into a
tyranny. Hence it is fitting that statesmen guard against the
coming-forth in cities of such a class as this even more than
the physician's precautions against the production of bad
humors in bodies. When they detect that something of them
25 comes forth in cities, they [must] tear them out by their
roots and cast them out of the city just as the physician does
with the two biles and the phlegm. This is even more fitting
for the statesman. This class of humans—i.e., those who
control everything that they desire—does not come into
being [alone] in this city. It is found, rather, that, as Plato
says, three classes of humans emerge in it. Their coming-
forth in it is the most helpful of things for its changing into
30 tyranny. As for the first class among them, that is the class
of drones whom we have characterized, those who abandon
[themselves] to all their desires. This class, as we have said,
96. are the honored and praised lords in this city. | There is also
a class that grows in this city that is abhorred in it, namely
that which loves money alone. The coming-forth of this
class in this city is as honey for these drones who eat it with
great speed. As for the third class, they are the people who

95.23   statesmen] Plato 564c: legislator.

keep to their own affairs or have no affairs, [and] they are ⊢
not wealthy. The moneyed kind, however, is persecuted in ⁵⁶⁵
5 this city; and these two classes combine to plunder ⌐and
rob them⌐ of their property, except that the first class does
this by way of desire and licentiousness, while the second
does this ⌐only⌐ because of the advancement they intend
for themselves by means of [the others'] property. That
advancement corresponds to the extent that those who seize
lordship of the association in this city find it possible to
plunder these of their property and to divide it among the
populace.

He said: The propertied are necessarily wronged by
these; and there arise here contentions and acts of violence
10 and robberies. It is the way of the populace to turn over
⌐their affairs⌐ to the one who is greatest in that class—i.e.,
of the people who give rein to their desires—and they
sustain him and make him great. Such an individual as this
does not cease adding gradually to [this] change and to
excess in freedom to the point that they enslave the majority
of the citizens and become thorough tyrants. The beginning
of the transformation of this one who ⌐comes⌐ to tyrannical
15 lordship from democratic lordship is this: When he begins
this lordship he commits tyrannical acts to the point that
he finally turns into a thorough tyrant. For on finding the
populace at the outset submissive to him in harming
whomever he wishes to harm and punishing him with
something detestable, and in destroying whomever he
wishes to destroy, he thus does not cease ⌐to bring⌐ one kind
of people into tyranny over another kind. And this, as we ⊢
have said, is so that the [different] kinds existing in this city ⁵⁶⁶

96.4   and] Following Plato 565a; MSS: except that.
96.12   change and . . . freedom] The change consists in depriving
the propertied of their political and economic importance. The freedom
is not for the citizens generally, but for the leader himself and for his
fellow drones.

be made evident, and particularly the moneyed kind, which
20 are the most hated of things in this city. He does not cease
doing this continuously until he becomes the enemy of most
of the citizens and hates them. Then, either they conspire
against him and kill him, or he rules over them and
tyrannizes them all and becomes a tyrant. (You yourself can
understand this clearly from this democratic lordship that
exists in our time for it often changes into tyranny. An
example of this is the lordship existing in this land of
25 ours—i.e., Córdoba—after 500 [A.H. = 1106]. It was almost
completely democratic; then the situation turned after 540
[= 1145] into a tyranny.)

As to how his rise comes about through these actions, and
what his governance comes to in the end, and the extent
of what befalls the city through him by way of injury and
evil, and the misfortune that befalls him himself, why that
will be made clear through speech and investigation. Plato
30 says that it is characteristic of this individual that he subdue
all humans and arouse them to hold fast to the nomos so
97. that it might be thought that he is not tyrannizing, | and
that he intends the guidance and direction of the citizens
[with a view] to dividing property and goods among them,
and that he has no other intention than the care of the
association and the improvement of the city. When he has
made peace with the enemies without by setting things
right with some and ⌜overcoming⌝ others, he turns to his
city where he continually stirs up wars among them. This
is so that he might control the property of its citizens and
5 seize it. For he holds that once he has plundered them of
their wealth they will be unable to shake him off, and they   567
will be preoccupied with themselves and with seeking their
daily bread, as happened to the people of our district with

96.24-26 See 92.4-8, above.

the individual known as Ibn Ghāniya. If it also comes into his mind to be frightened of people in the populace on account of their having much wealth and substantial possessions and power, he cunningly devises their destruction by turning them over to their enemies. Similarly, he ⌐hates⌐ whatever human is of this description among his peers and
10 whom he has made into his henchmen. When ⌐he⌐ does these actions, the greatest thing is [his] hatred of the citizens. That is why he makes use of his energy to recognize these—i.e., men of might, courage, and greatness—among them. He plots against them until he purges the city ⌐of them⌐. This purge is the opposite of the purge by which the physicians purge bodies and the wise [purge] the virtuous cities; for these extract the worst and cast it out, while this one does the opposite. That is why the tyrant is obliged to
15 be in one of two conditions: either not to live, or to dwell with evil and sinful people who hate him. This is one thing in which, according to him, the tyrant takes delight. Undoubtedly, as long as he engages in these actions and his enmity toward his citizens grows, he will have need of more numerous henchmen so that he may be more protected and secure. This can only be provided for him if he engages evil foreigners, to the exclusion of the citizens; he draws them
20 ⌐from every⌐ place ⌐if⌐ he gives them pay. These are his trusted friends, and he destroys those predecessors who set him up as ruler of the association. If the tyrant finds nothing ⊢

568de

97.7   One of a family that were prominent opponents of the Almohad dynasty and leaders in the attempted restoration of Almoravid rule in North Africa.

97.7-8   Plato 567a: if he suspects certain men of having free thoughts and not putting up with his ruling.

97.15-16   Plato 567d: either dwell with the ordinary many, even though hated by them, or cease to live.

97.21   Averroes passes over, for the moment, the digression in Plato 568a–c wherein the tragic poets are attacked for their praise of tyranny. See 101.15-18, below.

with which to feed this army and camp, the situation will compel him—should there be any wealth in the city in one of the temples—to order that it be taken out. Similarly, he conspires against the property of the association that set
25 him up as one of the ⌜democratic⌝ rulers. As this activity of his against the association increases, they see that this ⌜is the opposite of what they intended⌝ in handing over the lordship to him, since they only intended by this that he 569 guard [them] from the rich and the gentlemen and other citizens once he possessed dominion and power, so that they might exist under his governance and the governance of his servants. Hence the association of the distressed ⌜then⌝ seek
30 to drive him out of their city, and he is compelled to enslave them and to take [their] arms from them. The condition of
98. the association with him is ⌜like⌝ what is said | in the metaphor of the torch burning over coals in the fire, for the association flees from some [sort of] servitude in handing over the lordship to him and falls [thereby] into an [even] harsher servitude. All these actions of the tyrants are manifest in this time of ours not only through argument but also through sense and evidence. We have spoken of the
5 manner in which the democratic city changes into the tyrannical city, and what is the condition of the citizens in a tyranny, and the extent of their distress.

Now we ought to consider ⌜also⌝ the individual who resembles this city, and how he changes from the individual 571 who is one of the democratic rulers, and whether his way of life in grief and lack of happiness resembles the governance of the city that is being tyrannized. We say that since

97.25 MS *A*: they see that this is the way in which they went astray.
97.26-27 the gentlemen] Literally: the virtuous and the good.
98.1 I.e., that in seeking to avoid the discomfort of the torch's smoke, men have been exposed to the greater hazard of being burned in the fire.
98.6 Paragraphing supplied.

Plato defined this individual as being, according to him, the
individual filled with unnecessary desires, he began by first
10 making known what these desires are. Then, after that, he
turns to describe the manner in which the tyrannical
individual is changed from an individual who exercises
democratic rule, and the extent of his grief and lack of
happiness, and [shows] that in this he resembles [the city]
that is being tyrannized. He said that the unnecessary
desires are those that are aroused and brought into motion
in sleep: i.e., the bestial part, when the cogitative part that
rules over this part is asleep. ⌈For⌉ it is the way of the bestial
⌈part⌉ during sleep, when released from the rule of the
15 cogitative part and from every ⌈thought⌉, that it holds at
that moment ⌈that nothing will frighten it off⌉ from seizing
what it desires when it awakens. When this part is brought
low by the nomoi [and] the better [desires], much of it is
nullified; and if some remnant of it remains, it is weak. But
if a man attends to this part [sc., the bestial part], his
condition in sleep does not resemble that of that first one.
Rather, this one's cogitative part in sleep is just as it is in ⊢—
waking so that he entertains no thought [hostile] to the ⁵⁷²
20 nomoi. Hence this resembles ⌈the two⌉ [kinds of] people,
the bestial and the divine. When it became clear to him
what the unnecessary desires are, he turned to investigate
what this individual—i.e., the tyrant—changes out of, and
said: We have already said of the democratic individual,
whom we mentioned in the preceding, that he is a young
fellow who grew up with a disposition to choose none of the
unnecessary desires apart from the accumulation of wealth.
Since this young fellow grew up among people filled with

98.16   Following Plato 571b; MSS: by the better nomoi.
98.19   hostile] Following Plato 572b. The MSS read: near to the
nomoi. The MSS may reflect an earlier mistranslation of the Greek
prefix *para* as "near" or "beside," which was taken over by Averroes.

25 ⌜un⌝necessary desires, and his nature was better than their
nature, and his father was drawing him toward his way of
life and they toward its opposite, he turns into something
intermediary between those two kinds and takes from each
one of them what to his mind is equitable. His way of life is
neither the way of life of one who has no freedom nor the
way of life of one who transgresses the nomos, and he is
transformed from being one belonging to the lordship of the
few to turn into one of the populace.

30   He said: All this being as we have characterized it, let it
be presupposed now that when one of this description
99. reaches | old age, he has a son who has grown up with his
disposition. Also let it be presupposed that those things that
happened to his parent happened to him—i.e., through
people whose way it is to draw ⌜him⌝ to that which has
[hostility] to the nomos—and that they lead him to utter
freedom. [Presuppose too] that his father, contrary to what
was the case with himself, has already attended in some way
to the birth of these desires [in the son], as also do his
5 servants and his relatives. He undoubtedly changes toward
excess in these desires more intently than did his father
because he has no one drawing him toward the other
extreme and because he finds no people to force him and to
oppose him. Rather he finds people who act cunningly
toward him regarding whatever it is that he loves. This one
[love] they place over all the desires, and it rules over them.
They [sc., the desires] make it [sc., the love] into what ⊢—
10 corresponds to one of the greatest drones in the hive. ⌜For 573
when he encounters the unnecessary desires⌝ such as
drunkenness from wines and incense and perfumed oils, and
in general all the delights [to be found] in [such] gatherings,

98.27 no freedom] Plato 572d: illiberal.
99.3 hostility] Following Plato 572e; MSS: nearness. See note to
98.19, above.

they depart from him and are utterly removed from him.
These drones are to be seen among them [sc., the unnecessary desires], and they hinder him to the point that his
mind is unbalanced and his excitement is intensified. Then
the demons seize him; and his confusion is intensified, and
he is beside himself ⌜if there remains in him⌝ some remnant
of [his earlier] life after all that has befallen ⌜him⌝ on
15 account of these desires. As this is the situation of the
tyrant—i.e., the situation of one who takes no notice,
neither little nor much, of the noblest of his parts, namely
reason—the situation of the tyrant resembles the situation
of the deranged and of the drunk, and his intellect resembles
his; and hence his status and position are similar to those of
the deranged and the drunk. Hence, unbalanced ones such
as these wish not merely for dominion over people, but over
angels too if this were only possible for them. This, then, is
20 the character of the tyrannical individual and the manner
by which he changes from the individual who is a democratic ruler. He only comes to such a condition as this after all
these things have befallen him [owing to his] nature and
way of life. When he completed this, he undertook to
consider the manner of this one's life and lordship. And he
said: This individual has gatherings based on the pleasures,
among which are bazaars, baths, and promenades, and in
general whatever causes love to dwell and arouses [erotic]
desire, which [in turn] overpowers him and guides the parts
25 of his soul just as the captain guides the ship. As this is the
situation of this individual, other desires will not cease being
aroused alongside these desires, just as ⌜the shoot⌝ sprouts

99.11   they depart] The referent is ambiguous. Averroes seems to be
referring to any vestiges of moderation in the young fellow.

99.19   angels] Plato 573c: gods.

99.27   Averroes' elaboration. Plato 573d speaks of desires sprouting
up beside the soul.

⌜at the side⌝ of the tree. He will have need of great expenditures; and if he has wealth, he spends it immediately.
Thus he soon has need of [further] expenditures, and
thereafter there arises for him the need to borrow from
30 others. Along with all this, his desire forces him to what is
beyond his capability, and particularly the erotic and
amatory desire, which are the guides of the rest of his
100. desires. | In general, he does not leave off the subject of his ⌞
desires, as Plato says, like one who indulges himself in
raising pigeons. Hence, only one of two things is possible
for him: either he draws toward himself whatever he wishes
from whatever place, or he feels pain as a woman feels pain
during her menstrual period or as an invalid in pain. If his ⌜
parents have something [left], he does not find what they   574
gave him to be sufficient, and he asks it of them. If they
5 refuse, he takes it from them, either by deception or by
theft or by force. If they still hinder him in this, he attends
to tyrannizing over them or killing them, as we see this
happening to many humans in these cities. This, then, is the
situation of one to whom a tyrannical child is born, who
finally comes to tyrannize his parent. His desires further
lead him to plunder houses of assembly and temples and
10 wayfarers. In general, those desires do not cease, but go on
increasing ⌜in him⌝ forever; they are intensified by the
dominion of [erotic] desire and love to the point that he
feels troubled. When he is relieved of the good ⌜opinions⌝
held by him from the period of his youth—at which time
his parent was raising him and he [sc., the son] was one of
the democrats—it reaches the point that his waking becomes, as Plato says, like his condition when asleep. He

100.1-2 Averroes' elaboration. Plato 573e speaks of a crowded nestful
of intense desires raising a clamor.
100.12-13 democrats] or: he was one of the democratic rulers. Plato
574e: there was a democratic regime in him.

denies himself nothing, and nothing frightens him. When ⊢
15 the likes of these drones multiply in democratic cities, they 575a–
575d
recognize that they [are a multitude]. They, with the help
also of the foolish populace, take the mightiest and strongest
of them in tyranny and deliver the lordship to him; and he
tyrannizes over them. Just as he formerly ruined father and
mother, so does he now ruin ⌐the city⌐ of his father and
forefather. If these drones are few in the city and if the
virtuous among them [sc., the citizens] rebuke them, then
the mightiest of them take to leaving the city and stand on
the roads robbing men of their lives and wealth.   ⊢

20 He said: It is the way with the tyrant's might that he does 576
not mark any of the citizens with love or affection that is
genuine or mutual. All this being as we have characterized
it, why then the governance of the tyrant is the governance
of utmost injustice since it is most contrary to that which
we previously defined to be the right one. It is this that is
of the utmost evil and ruination, just as what preceded
25 concerning the king is of the utmost goodness and excellence. Since the situation as among cities is like the situation
as among individuals, there is, therefore, no one more happy
than the virtuous king and no one more wretched than the
tyrant. This comparison between each one of them—i.e., ∟
the comparison of city to city and individual to individual—
is, however, clearer in [the case of] the city. This being so,
if we ourselves accept that the relation of city to city is [the
30 same as] the relation of individual to individual, then this
comparison between the two of them—i.e., between the
101. two people—becomes clear. | Hence the accidents and
properties characteristic of this city ought to be reflected
upon, and we must judge the tyrant in the light of them.
It is clear that this city is in extreme slavery and very far ⌐
removed from freedom. Similarly, the soul of the tyrant is 577c–
577e

100.15 Following Plato 575c to fill a lacuna in the Hebrew text.

filled with slavery and devoid of freedom; for the base part
5 rules over it, while the parts that are of utmost fitness are
enslaved. When a city is enslaved, either it does not bring
about what it wishes or else brings about only little of it;
hence they are full of sighing, sorrow, and mourning. As for ⊢—
those filled with tyranny, it is also clear from their situation 578a
that they are impoverished. Similarly, the tyrannical soul
is impoverished, not sated.

He said: And just as this city is in utmost fear, so is the
10 tyrant. And just as there is not to be found in any city more
mourning and weeping than in this city, so is the case with
the tyrant's soul, which is filled with persistent desires and
unfulfilled loves. This, then, is what Plato said in com- ⌞
paring these cities and these people. But since he found this
comparison, which we have described, between the virtuous
city and the tyrannical one clearer than that between the
two people ruling over them, he wished to make the case
15 of the tyrant manifest through a clear example. [He does]
all this on account of the renown of ⌜tyrannical⌝ lordship in
his time, and the poems in praise of them, and their
assertion that it is the lordship of the free. I have seen many
among the poets and those who grow up in these cities who
prefer this lordship They hold that it is the ultimate end
and that there is excellence in the tyrannical soul, and they
hold fast to [this] lordship. He resumed and said that it is ⌜
clear that the relation of the tyrant to those over whom he 578de
20 tyrannizes is the relation of the master to the slave. If we
presuppose that there is a rich individual who has many
slaves and who does them no good at all, this can only be
because the nonslave citizens among the people of his
homeland are twice the number of the slaves. Now if we

101.15-18 Averroes picks up the theme of Plato 568a–c, which he
passed over at 97.21.

101.16 grow up] Other MSS: many of the poets who grow up.

presuppose that such an individual as this, and his children,
wives, and property, are in a certain region of the earth
where there is none other than slaves with him and where,
in general, he is in a situation in which it would be impossible for someone without freedom to help him, why then
owing to his slaves he necessarily reaches [a state] of great
25 ⌜fear⌝ for his wives, property, children, and himself. The ⊢
situation compels him to deliver up his slaves or [at least] 579
some of them. Although there is no obligation ⌜to do this⌝,
he accumulates many things for them and withholds them
from himself so as to bind them [to him]. He will be in one
of two conditions: either great strength accrues to him, or
he comes to lose any importance. If, moreover, God were
to place people ⌜around him⌝ who hold that there is no
necessity that one have lordship over another, would not
the heart of this individual grow faint and would he not be
102. among them ⌜as though he were⌝ under detention? | This
is necessarily the situation of the tyrant: he is detained
among a class such as this, filled with hunger and fear.
Moreover, he has great hunger ⌜within⌝ himself and cannot
rule himself. Hence he cannot go wherever he wishes nor
look at whatever he wishes, but rather ⌜only⌝ lives the life
of a woman. One of the worst dispositions of such an
5 individual is that he is unable to restrain and overcome
himself, yet he attempts to lead other people at some level.
It is as if a man who is sick in all his bodily dispositions, as
much as he reckons on curing what [ails] him, leaves off
curing his body and [instead] improves his property as far
as is possible for him and takes to healing [other] people's
bodies in accord with his notions. On account of all this,
the tyrant is the most enslaved of people and has no device

101.24   great fear] Following Plato 578e, one MS, and Mantinus;
other MSS: great calamity.
102.9-10   Or: no device for the longing of his desires.

10 by which to put an end to his desires, but rather is forever
in continual sorrow and mourning. The soul of one who is
of this description is an impoverished soul; hence he is
envious, violent, and friendless. These states having existed
in him prior to his lordship, they are even more necessary
after [he assumes] the lordship. Without any doubt, he is of
necessity troubled and unlucky, for he who rides chance and
accident often comes to lose any importance. All this, as we
have said ⌜more than once⌝, is clear and may be discerned
15 through argument as well as through the sense[s]. From the
sum of this argument have been made evident the order
[of succession] of these cities, the happiness and misfortune
in them, the order of those ruling over them, and that the
happiest of them is the king just as the most unfortunate of
them is the tyrant. This, then, is what Plato holds concerning the change of these cities and of the people in them
one into another.

One might object and say that if the case is as he thought,
20 namely that there is among these cities ⌜what⌝ resembles
⌜two opposites—the two being⌝ the virtuous city and the
tyrannical one—and that there is among them what resembles an intermediary between the extremes, then it does
not necessarily follow that the change of cities proceeds
according to [this] order. This exists only in natural things,
for it is the way with nature to bring about opposites via
intermediaries. As for these things, they are completely

(right margin, lines 9–13) ⊢ 580a-580c

(right margin, line 18) ⌐

102.11   friendless] Plato 580a: envious, faithless, unjust, friendless,
impious, and a host and nurse for all vice; and, thanks to all this,
unlucky in the extreme.

102.13   unlucky] The following clause is Averroes' addition, as is the
subsequent sentence.

102.15   argument] or: from the contents of this treatise. Averroes
omits Plato's repetition of the five types of cities and men.

102.19   Paragraphing supplied.

voluntary. And [since] all these natures—i.e., the natures
we have described—are to be found in all these cities, it is
25 possible for any city among them to change into any other.
We say that what Plato said ⌐undoubtedly⌐ is not necessary,
but ⌐it is⌐ [this way] as a rule. The cause of this is that the
governance that is laid down has an effect by transferring
certain states [of the soul] to whoever grow up in it, even if
these are opposite to what is fixed in the nature of those who
are being disposed toward those states. It is possible thereby
for the majority of people to excel in the human virtues.
30 This is only rarely impossible. This has already been made
clear in the first part of this science, for it was stated there
that the way of attaining the practical virtues is habitude,
just as the way of attaining the theoretical sciences is study. |
103. This being so, man's transformation from one state to
another is consequent upon the transformation of the laws
and ⌐is arranged according to their order⌐. Since the nomoi,
and especially in the virtuous city, are not suddenly transformed—and this too is because of the habits and excellent
states to which they accustom its members and with which
5 they grow up—but rather are only transformed gradually
and to what is proximate [to them, it follows that] the
transformation in habits and dispositions necessarily changes
according to that order, to the point that when the laws are
utterly corrupted, the states [of the soul] existing there will
be utterly base. You can make this clear from what—after
forty years—has come about among us in the habits and

102.23 voluntary] See discussion of voluntary intelligibles and the
deliberative faculty in Farabi, *Attainment*, 17.17-28.4 (*MPP*, pp. 62-68).

102.26 as a rule] The earlier discussion of the transformation of
regimes was cast in terms of possibilities and likelihoods, rather than
inexorable necessities. See 89.32-90.4, 92.12, 93.6-8, 93.18-21, above.

102.28 It is possible thereby] I.e., by transferring certain states of
the soul to the inhabitants (given the virtuous city or excellent laws).

102.30-31 Aristotle *Nicomachean Ethics* 2. 1. 1103a14–b25.

103.8-12 "Forty years" appears to refer to the period beginning with

states of those possessing lordship and status. Because the
10 timocratic governance under which they grew up has been
undone, they have come by these base things that they now
have. Only he among them who is virtuous according to the
Legal prescriptions remains in an excellent state. This is
rare among them. When Plato completed this he wished
also to compare the pleasures occurring to each one of these
because this belongs to the completion of the comparison
between them. With this he completes his discourse con-
15 cerning the necessary parts of this science, and this is what
we ourselves had in mind to explain.

⌈He began and he said:⌉ Since the states of the soul are   ⌈
comprised within three classes, so too are the kinds of cities. 580d–581
The first kind is that which loves wisdom; the second is that
which loves mastery—if in moderation, then it is honor
[-loving], and if in excess it is victory[-loving]; and the
third, the appetitive one, is ⌈that which⌉ loves gain. The
kinds of pleasures are necessarily [also] three, [one] for each
of these, since it is clear from the character of the pleasures
20 that they are an appendant shadow.

Plato began by using a dialectical argument to explain
which of these pleasures is most worthy of choice. For ⌈he
said⌉ that every one of the adherents of these three pleasures
is found to choose only the pleasure incidental to his way
of life. Thereafter he laid down a well-known topic from
among those mentioned in ⌈Book II of the⌉ *Topics*, namely
25 the Book of Dialectic. He said that what the man of wisdom
and knowledge chooses is most worthy of choice. And he
reinforced this topic by saying that the man of wisdom ⌈and ⊢
knowledge⌉ is he who has two instruments by him whereby 582

the establishment of the present (i.e., Almohad) rule ca. 1146. The
decay in that regime has already been alluded to by Averroes in 89.31
and 92.7-8, above.
    103.17, 18   moderation, excess] Averroes' additions.

things are arranged in order, namely experience and reasoning. To the man of wisdom alone does it befall that he arranges
these three pleasures in order through experience and
reasoning. As for experience, that is because he has tasted
those pleasures from the time of his youth; but these others
104. do not | taste at all the delight of wisdom. As for the man of
wisdom being the one for whom it is possible to proceed
through argument and reasoning, why this is self-evident. For ⊢
we see that the multitude remember the pleasures ⌈only⌉ at 583cd
the time when their opposites are joined to them, ⌈so that⌉
when they are ill they say that health is the most pleasant
5 of things, ⌈and in time of poverty they say that wealth is the
most pleasant of things⌉. But things pleasant do not require, ⌊
as such, being preceded by an opposite. An example of this
is vision, and so on. Indeed, the noblest of pleasures are
those that are other than of this character and hence exist
more fully. Plato elaborated upon this intention—i.e., the
ignorance of whoever would be the equal of the wise in
judging the pleasures, and the capability of the wise to do
10 this. Yet with all this, the argument does not rise to being
demonstrative; so we leave it and take up what he says of
this later on, which does appear to be demonstrative for
he made use therein of another argument, and this is it.

He said: Just as hunger and thirst are an emptying of the ⌈
body and an emptiness that befalls it, so are ignorance and 585
absence of knowledge an emptying of the soul and an
emptiness for it. This being so, there are two people who
are filled—i.e., he who takes food and he who acquires
knowledge. But the true fullness is only through the thing
15 that has the noblest existence, namely that which [partici-
pates] most in being and most in truth. Things ⌈only⌉ excel

104.4-5 Averroes adds the example of poverty and wealth. See
Aristotle *Nicomachean Ethics* 1. 4. 1095a24 f.
104.6   vision] Plato 584b: the pleasures of smells in particular.

in this matter according to their proximity to, or remoteness from, the eternal things, which truly exist and endure permanently. This being so, the thing whereby the souls are filled [participates] more in truth than the thing that fills the body since the soul is closer to the eternal things than
20 is the body, especially if the apprehension of their form is an eternal apprehension. Now if, in general, fullness in what one apprehends is pleasant, whatever ⌜he apprehends of what⌝ is essentially nobler and [participates] more in truth and is more enduring, is necessarily a more choiceworthy pleasure. Such is the case of the pleasure of the intellect ⌞ relative to the other pleasures. For ⌜those⌝ pleasures perish rapidly because opposites are mixed in with them, while the pleasure of the intellect has no opposite. Thus either it
25 is eternal, or it perishes owing to a change that comes over it. And this argument—upon my life!—is a demonstrative argument.

Furthermore, he also said: As for most of the pleasures of the intellect, they become better as the intellect performs them. Whatever is the cause of something's being in the best condition is itself more choiceworthy. This being so, it is the judge who attains all the pleasures to the greatest extent possible. And this—upon my life!—is the truth, except for the statement wherein ⌜he said⌝ that whatever is the cause
30 of something's being of the best character is itself better. That is [merely] a generally accepted argument, although
105. he does not explain it. | Galen, in his ignorance of logical methods, thinks that these are all demonstrative arguments. But of these arguments comparing these pleasures, the only demonstrative argument is that argument alone which precedes this one.

104.23-28 Plato *Philebus* 52b, 55a, 59c, 64d–65a.
104.28 Or: it [sc., the intellect] is the judge who understands all the pleasures in the best possible way.

This, then—may God preserve your honor and prolong
your days!—is the sum of the scientific arguments necessary
5 for this part of [political] science as are contained in these
arguments attributable to Plato. We have explained them
as briefly as we possibly could on account of the troubles of
the time. This was only attainable for us because of your
helping us to understand them and because of the boon of
your ⌜sharing⌝ in all that we have longed for of these
sciences and your helping us toward them with the most
complete kind of help. You are the cause not only of this
good being bestowed upon, and transferring to us, but also
10 of whatever human goods we have acquired, which God
(may He be exalted!) has bestowed upon us for your sake.
May God preserve your honor!

What the tenth treatise encompasses is not necessary for
this science. For at its beginning he explains that the art
of poetry has neither the purpose nor the knowledge from
which true knowledge comes about. This matter has already
been completely explained elsewhere. Then he mentions
thereafter a rhetorical or dialectical argument by which he
15 explains that the soul ⌜does not⌝ die. Then there is a story
after that in which he describes the bliss and delight that
await the souls of the happy and the just, and what awaits
the souls of the tormented. We have ⌜made it known more
than once⌝ that these stories are of no account, for the
virtues that come about from them are not true virtues. If
one calls them virtues, it is [only] homonymously. They
belong to the remote imitations. This has already preceded

105.4   Rosenthal, p. 300, tentatively identifies the addressee as the
Almohad ruler, Abū Yaʿqūb Yūsuf (reigned 1163-1184). Teicher
(p. 193), conjectures that the addressee is, rather, Abū Yaʿqūb's son
and successor, Abū Yūsuf Yaʿqūb al-Manṣūr (reigned 1184-1198/99).
The date of this work's composition is not known.

105.11   Paragraphing supplied.

105.16-17   not true virtues] Consider 31.7-25, above.

in [the discussion of] the genus of imitations. It is this that
has brought us to an untruth such as this. It is not something
20 necessary to a man's becoming virtuous, nor will it be better
and easier for a man to become virtuous through it. For we
see here many people who, in adhering to their nomoi and
their Laws, albeit devoid of these stories, are not less well off
than those possessing [these] stories. In general, there is in
these stories that over which the ancients had already
disputed; and Plato was troubled thereby. ⌜What they⌝
25 [sc., these stories] are is clear from ⌜his discourse⌝ at the
beginning of this book. As for the first treatise of this book,
they are entirely dialectical arguments; there is no demonstration in them other than by accident. Similarly with the
opening of the second; hence we do not explain anything
of what is in it. May God help you with that which you are
presently undertaking; and, in His will and holiness, may
He remove the obstacles.

The treatise is completed, and with its completion the
explanation is completed. Praise be to God!

105.25   And with this Averroes excuses himself from giving an account of Plato's theory of the immortality of the soul. Farabi, too, ends
his summary of Plato's *Laws* with Book IX.

105.28-29   Paragraphing supplied. Teicher ascribes these lines to a
copyist.

Appendixes

APPENDIX I

Translator's Colophon

Averroes' explanation of the scientific arguments found in Plato's *Republic* is completed; this is the beginning of the second part of political science. Its translation was completed on 22 Kislev 5081 (after the Creation) [= 24 November 1320] in the city of Uzès. I, Samuel ben Judah ben Meshullam ben Isaac ben Solomon, Barbevaire, of Marseilles, translated it.[1] When I was translating it there had not come into my hands Averroes' explanation of the philosopher Aristotle's *Ethics*, which is the first part of this volitional science, but only the Philosopher's statements themselves. I was unable to translate them owing to their profundity and their difficulty. I applied myself to this and strove mightily until there came into my hands the explanation of that part by the aforementioned scholar, Averroes, [written] in distinct, clear language as is his fine way in all of his explanations. I aroused myself to translate it; and God, honored in His mercifulness, approved of my doing so as a good thing so that the translation of the explanations of the whole of political science was completed. Then I went over the whole of my translation of this science and

[1] There is an account of Samuel ben Judah's life and works by Lawrence V. Berman, in Alexander Altmann (ed.), *Jewish Medieval and Renaissance Studies*, Philip W. Lown Institute of Advanced Judaic Studies, Brandeis University, Studies and Texts, vol. 4 (Cambridge: Harvard University Press, 1967), pp. 289-303. Berman's translations of these two colophons appear on pp. 307-311 and p. 311, n. 36. In translating I follow the Hebrew text of Samuel's colophon as published in E. I. J. Rosenthal (ed. and trans.), *Averroes' Commentary on Plato's "Republic"* (Cambridge: Cambridge University Press, 1956, 1966, 1969), pp. 106-107; by permission of Cambridge University Press. The copyist's colophon is that of MS *A*.

corrected the errors as best I could. The work of careful examination and improvement was completed on 26 Elul of that year [= 20 September 1321] in the chateau at Beaucaire, [where I was] confined and abandoned with more of our brethren, and shut up in one of its fortifications called the Redoubt. It is not impossible, but rather possible, even certain, that he who considers this translation of mine of the two parts of this science will be in doubt concerning some of its passages because of my poor translation owing to my inadequate grasp of the Arabic language. But—by the worship!—I hereby expect and trust that those errors will be excused for their paucity; they are not far off from what is customarily [encountered] in the translation of other books ascribable to one or another of the translators who came before me. Perhaps hereafter, by decree of heaven, one of the select few who are expert in both languages will be emboldened and aroused with firm heart and fresh spirit to remove and clear out my mistakes and errors so that the translation of this science be perfected. I, out of my love for it and diligence in it, thought of and imagined going even further by improving this translation together with Christian scholars; and especially the first part of it, for the statements of the Philosopher on that part are to be found among them as well as interpretation of them by Abū Naṣr al-Fārābī. By the Law and the testimony![2] As I had imagined [it], so would it have been, had not the cause alluded to, concerning the long and harsh imprisonment that occurred to us at this time, hindered me from [doing] this. If God prolongs my life and brings me out—a prisoner from the dungeon, out of the prison-house[3]—and offers me the briefest leisure, I will attempt this. I will go further in inquiry and research, from the beginning of the science to its end, in orderly fashion, until the translation is brought to the most perfect state. Hence, until this is accomplished, let him who studies this science not blame me on coming

[2] Cf. Isa. 8:20.
[3] Cf. Isa. 42:7.

to passages where there are mistakes and errors. For there is no man who never fails,[4] nor is there a craftsman who does not err in his work on rare occasions. All the more, then, with practitioners of the craft of translation, which is burdensome and difficult work. For the craftsman in it needs to be expert in both of the languages—i.e., that from which he translates and that into which he translates—and be a scholar, not only of the science or art that he is translating, but of all or most generally known sciences as well, since all the sciences and arts are intertwined with one another, for the one is always being compared to the others. The early translators who came before us had already drawn attention to this or something like it in their apologies for their translations. Notwithstanding the great perplexities, confusions, and injuries that have befallen our people and that for a long time have come continuously one after another—the latest [of these misfortunes] being the most calamitous—whatever of this art has come our way at the present time is excellent. Let us praise God (may He be exalted!) and give Him great thanks for having helped us in this. In general, I say: You men of speculation, oh community of believers in the truth! May His way be accomplished! Give credit to whomever it is due! For to this very day, nothing at all of this science has been translated or has come down to us, neither from the Philosopher nor from others, except for whatever of this is to be found in the *Book of the Principles of the Beings*[5] by Abū Naṣr al-Fārābī, which has fallen into the hands of many of the people of our nation. This has only some of the second part of this science; there is nothing in it of the first part. I myself was emboldened to begin to show the honor of this science's glorious majesty[6] and to bring it forth in our language. Even if the good that exists in it is slight owing to my shortcomings, here is the treatise as a start. Even if

[4] Cf. I Kings 8:46 and II Chron. 6:36.
[5] *The Political Regime.*
[6] Cf. Esther 1:4.

it is slight, it is potentially great.[7] However that may be, sleepers, awake from the deep sleep of slothfulness and the ignorance that is devoid of any positive quality; [it is that] which leads and brings down [the ignorant] into the nethermost pit [and] which passes by and loses complete happiness.[8] Awake, ye who are drunk with troubles; rejoice greatly.[9] Take hold of this fair portion that God has allotted you. Hear, ye deaf, what these two divine kings have spoken; look, ye blind, and see the light that is bright in the skies.[10] Surely seek counsel; who created all these exalted wonders, elevated beyond all praise? Look into the vision; behold, your reward is with you and your recompense before you.[11]

The translator said: I had resolved to improve the translation of this science together with Christian scholars but was unable to do so owing to the force of the expulsions and imprisonments that befell us from this people, which banishes us. We were a proverb and a taunt among them; they made us like the dust in threshing.[12] Yet I was scrupulous in inquiry concerning it; and wherever I was in doubt I always consulted the book of the Philosopher and, as best I could, made what was crooked straight. This is how I conducted myself with respect to the *Ethics*, but in the case of the *Republic* I had no other book. Nonetheless, I am sure that my errors in it are few and that he who looks into this after me will make amends for me and judge me with an inclination in my favor, as befits the sect of those who philosophize, seekers of the true reality of knowledge in beings.[13]

[7] Steinschneider: "so scheint er gross im Verhältnis zur Fähigkeit des Autors" (*Hebr. Üb.*, p. 223).
[8] Cf. Prov. 19:15 and Ps. 55:24.
[9] Cf. Joel 1:5 and Isa. 61:10.
[10] Cf. Isa. 42:18 and Job 37:21.
[11] Cf. Dan. 9:23 and Isa. 40:10.
[12] Cf. Jer. 24:9 and II Kings 13:7.
[13] Or (emending *amitūth* to *immūth*): seekers after the verification of knowledge in existing things.

This revision was completed in the month of Tammuz, 5082 [= June/July 1322]. Praised be the Creator who helped me, and may He be exalted forever! Amen.

Blessed be He who giveth power to the faint; and to him that hath no might He increaseth strength.[14]

Be strong!

Copyist's Colophon

The name of the thinker who translated this book—i.e., Aristotle's *Ethics* and the Platonic *Republic*—is Rabbi Samuel ben Judah ben Meshullam ben Isaac ben Solomon of Marseilles. It was he who translated it into the holy tongue and made many apologies of various kinds for the confusion in translation attending most of the *Ethics* and many parts of the Platonic *Republic*. It appears that this young fellow was expert in the holy tongue, but he was not perfected in forming a translation and [in] knowledge of the language from which he was translating. The honor due to him remains; and in any event we ought to praise him and acknowledge his industriousness in striving to provide us with a translation of this art, whether in respect of the goodness that is already in this book as it stands, or in respect of its being an incitement to set right its deficiency and give a proper shape to the whole of it (though the work involved is considerable). In any event, since we in our misery are mingled with the nations, we need to make use of their instruments whenever we happen to have any undertaking in common with them—until there comes He who purifies and refines silver,[15] in His mercy raising a poor and needy people out of the dust.

I, Moses ben Rabbi Isaac (may his soul be in Eden!) Rieti,

[14] Cf. Isa. 40:29.
[15] Cf. Mal. 3:3.

wrote [this copy of] this book, notwithstanding the deficiency in its translation, while seventy years old in my mortal life, which is the year 5217 [= 1457]. Not even this shall be wanting for my children, along with the rest of the books that I wrote and caused to be written and bought for them as I was free to do so, in addition to what my father and teacher (peace be on him!) wrote. May they find grace, good understanding in the eyes of God and man![16]

Selah!

[16] Cf. Prov. 3:4 and 13:15.

Notes to the Hebrew Text

In publishing the Hebrew text, Rosenthal chose not to produce a complete *apparatus criticus*, listing instead only those variants that he judged to be significant. I have compared his listing of variants only with MS *A*. I have here added to that list of variants by and large only in those cases where I follow MS *A* and where the unlisted variant results in a difference that is expressible in English. Such added readings are marked with an asterisk.

Also listed here are emendations of the Hebrew text, whether made by me or adopted by me from others, all of whom are identified by surname. Of the latter class of emendations, twenty appear in Rosenthal's *apparatus*.

Excerpts and paraphrastic renderings of this text occur in Joseph ben Shemtob's *Kebhod Elohim* (Ferrara, 1555). (Norman Golb drew my attention to the existence of such parallel passages and kindly lent me his copy of the work.) I note the following: 4a, 21-25 (*Kebhod Elohim*) = 65.9-14 (Rosenthal); 5a, 7-13, 15-18 = 67.8-15, 16-20; 5a, 25-5b, 10 = 67.20-68.11; 6a, 10-17, 22-24, 28-31 = 68.15-25, 69.12-14, 20-23; 6a, 32-6b, 1 = 71.25-28; 6b, 3-5 = 69.28-31; 6b, 6-7a, 3 = 72.1-32; 18b, 25-19a, 11 = 104.12-28. The variants from our text are on the whole slight.

22.18   human perfection] MS *A*: *beshlēmūth ha-enūshī* (sing.).*
28.17   love] Emending *ha-śin'ah*—hatred—to *ha-ahabhah*, following Caspi, Medigo, and Mantinus.

28.29   compared] Emending *dimyōnō* to *damīnū* (Rabin, cited in Rosenthal).

29.5   turning] Transposing *vyashūbhū bazeh* (Teicher).

30.7   divine acts] Reading *ha-pe'ulōth*, with MS *A* and Farabi, rather than *ha-mūśkalōth*.*

31.1   certain] Assuming an original *yushaqqu* misread by the Hebrew translator as *yūshiqu* (Baneth, cited in Rosenthal).

31.6   closely] *bedaqūth* (5 MSS). MS *A*: *bedatōth*–in religions (laws).

32.12   the righteous] Assuming an original *ṣāliḥūn* or *ṣulaḥā'* carried over into Hebrew as *ha-maṣliḥīm* (Vajda, cited in Rosenthal).

33.12   looks] Emending *vha-tmūrah*—and transformation— to *vha-tmūnah* (Rosenthal).

33.18   looks] Emending *betmūrah* to *betmūnah* (Rosenthal).

34.19   illustrious] Emending *sipūrēy* to *sefūnēy* or *safūn* (Mahdi). This is in accord with Mantinus.

35.28   the beautiful] MS *A*: *ha-ṭōbh*—the good.*

36.16   soft] Emending *ha-rabīm*—many—to *ha-rakhīm* (Rosenthal).

37.18   benefit] Emending *vha-hanaḥah* to *vha-hana'ah* (Mahdi).

37.26   a defect] Suppressing *qabhū'a*—chronic (Teicher).

37.27   come to grief] Emending MSS readings *vyibhshar* and *vyikhshar* to *vyikhshal* (Teicher).

39.8   most disciplined] Emending *vha-mūsar* to *vha-myūsar* (Teicher).

39.23   the dead] Emending *ha-mītah*—death—to *ha-mētīm* (Rabin, cited in Rosenthal).

41.25   need] Emending *derekh*—way—to *ṣōrekh* (Rosenthal).

42.12   with them] Emending *mēhem*—from them—to *'imam*.

44.3   citizens] MS *A*: *ba'alēy ha-medīnah*, rather than *ba'alēy ha-medīnōth*.*

44.27   loot] Emending *ha-klal* to *ha-shalal* (Rosenthal).

45.4   for the body] Assuming an original *min qibal* mistranslated as *miqōdem*—prior to (Berman).

45.18   become costly] Reading *she-yīqrū*, with MS *A*, rather than *she-yiqrū*.*

46.19   Lawgiver] Emending *ba'alēy* to *ba'al* (Vajda, cited in Rosenthal).

46.28   over them] Reading *'alēyhem*, with MS *A*, rather than *ēlēyhem*.*

53.22   deserts] Emending *al-barbarī* to *ha-barārī* (Baneth, cited in Rosenthal).

53.28   of the animals] Suppressing the conjunction in *ubebaʿaléy
        ḥayyim* (Teicher, cited in Rosenthal).

54.22   them] Reading *lahen* (fem.), with MS *A*, rather than *lahem*
        (masc.).*

55.21   in fact] Emending *beʿaṣmam* to *beʿeṣem* (Teicher, cited in Rosen-
        thal).

56.12-13 since] Assuming an original *idh* misread by the Hebrew
        translator as *wa-in* and translated as *af ʿal pi*—even though.

59.12   and kiss him] Emending *vyehargēhū*—and kill him—to *vyeḥabkēhū*
        (Teicher).

61.15   followed] Assuming an original *yuʾtammu* misread by the He-
        brew translator as *yuʾtamanu*—trusted (Kraus, cited in Rosen-
        thal).

64.5   badly] Assuming an original *sūʾ* misread by the Hebrew
        translator as *sawāʾ*—just (Mahdi).

64.11   thought] Emending *sibatham*—their cause—to *sbharatham*
        (Rosenthal).

65.7   necessarily] *hekhraḥ mah = darūratan mā*, rather than *darūrata mā*—
        does not know the necessity in that which leads to it (Mahdi).

65.27   infinite] Adding *biltī* (Strauss).

66.10   acquiring] Assuming an original *yattakhidhu* misread by the
        Hebrew translator *yattaḥidu*—to unite (Mahdi).

68.11   required by virtue] Following the reading: *lnefesh ha-medabereth
        kfi asher tḥayybhēhū ha-maʿalah*. This variant or elaboration ap-
        pears in the quotation of this passage by Joseph ben Shemtob,
        Kebhod Elohim, p. 5b.

69.25   justice] Reading *ha-shivūy*, with MS *A*, rather than *ha-shinūy*.*

69.26   necessarily] MS *A*: *behekhraḥ*.*

70.11   genus] Assuming an original *jins* misread by the Hebrew
        translator as *juzʾ*—part (Mahdi).

72.32   theoretical perfection] The quotation in Joseph ben Shemtob's
        Kebhod Elohim, p. 7a, continues: and that this is man's ultimate
        perfection and his end.

75.24   unknown] Emending *mūškaléy*—known—to *mūskaléy*, following
        Mantinus (Strauss).

76.27   generals] Assuming an original *quwwād* (Rabin, cited in
        Rosenthal).

78.6   he believed] Vocalizing a presumed *ya'taqidu* instead of *yu'taqadu* (Mahdi).

78.15   is provided with] MS *A*: *hayah yamṣī' mēhem.** This is in accord with Plato 540b.

78.22   expel them] Emending *vyaṣ'ū mēhem* to *vyōṣī'ūm* (Rosenthal).

80.29   speech] Assuming an original *bi'l-qawl* misread by the Hebrew translator as *bi'l-fi'l*—in deed (Mahdi).

82.6   Whoever] Emending *mimī* to *ūmī* (Teicher, cited in Rosenthal).

84.12   Note. MS *A*: *lo' yitakēn.**

87.20   it] Suppressing the conjunction in *vshehī'* (Rabin, cited in Rosenthal).

88.3   in particular] Assuming *sgulah* is a translation of *khāṣṣatan* (Pines).

89.8   he is not] Emending *shehū'*—that he is—to *sheēynō* (Rabin, cited in Rosenthal).

90.13   to him who has the capacity] MS *A*: *lmī shebō sēfeq.**

91.5   just as increase] MS *A*: *kmō sheyirbū.**

92.11   with the city] Emending *bemadrēgath*—the rank of—to *bemedīnath* (Strauss).

92.28   since . . . things] MS *A*: *aḥar shehēm lo' yashgīḥū bidbharīm.**

93.12   held] Emending *mithḥazēq* to *mūḥazaq.*

95.28   in it] MS *A*: *bah.**

96.27   comes to] Reading *she'ēlav*, with MS *A*, rather than *she'alav.**

97.23   one of the . . . rulers] MS *A*: *miba'alēy ha-adōnūth.**

98.1   over] Reading *'al*, with MS *A*, rather than *min.**

98.15   nothing] Emending *shesham*—that something is there—to *sheshūm.*

98.23   who grew up] MS *A*: *ṣamaḥ.**

100.2   for him] MS *A*: *lō.**

100.22-23 since . . . defined] MS *A*: *aḥar shehī' betakhlīth ha-hefekh lzeh asher gadarnūhū.**

101.26 obligation] Emending *ta'anah*—claim—to *to'an.*
        so as] Emending *vyiqshoram* to *lyiqshoram.*

103.3   are] Reading *shehayū*, with MS *A*, rather than *shehū'.**

103.17 mastery] Assuming an original *ghalaba* misread by the Hebrew translator as *ghāya*—end (Mahdi).

103.25 He said that] Suppressing *ela'.*

Short Titles and Editions Cited

This list is limited to Arabic and Hebrew texts and their translations that are cited in abbreviated form in the footnotes. Where there is a translation, it is listed immediately after the original-language work. P indicates that the translation is not of the entire work, but only of a part.

Avempace, *Governance*

Ibn Bājjah, *Tadbīr al-mutawaḥḥid, El Régimen del Solitario*, ed. and Spanish trans. by Miguel Asín Palacios (Madrid-Granada: Escuelas de Estudios Árabes, 1946).
The Governance of the Solitary, trans. Lawrence Berman, in *MPP*, pp. 122-133 (P).

Averroes, *Decisive Treatise*

Ibn Rushd, *Kitāb faṣl al-maqāl*, ed. George F. Hourani (Leiden: Brill, 1959). The page numbers of the *editio princeps* of Marcus Joseph Mueller, *Philosophie und Theologie von Averroes* (Munich, 1859), appear in the margins of this edition.
The Decisive Treatise, trans. George F. Hourani, in *MPP*, pp. 163-185.

———, *Exposition*

Kitāb al-kashf ʿan manāhij al-adilla ["Exposition of the Methods of the Proofs in the Dogmas of Religion"], in Marcus Joseph Mueller (ed.), *Philosophie und Theologie von Averroes*, Monumenta Saecularia, I. Classe, 3 (Munich, 1859), pp. 27-127. (German trans. in Mueller's book of the same title [Munich, 1875], pp. 26-118.)

———, *Incoherence*

Tahāfot at-tahāfot (Incohérence de l'Incohérence), ed. Maurice Bouyges,

Bibliotheca Arabica Scholasticorum, Série Arabe, vol. 3 (Beirut: Imprimerie Catholique, 1930).
Averroes' Tahafut al-tahafut (The Incoherence of the Incoherence), trans. Simon Van den Bergh, Unesco Collection of Great Works, Arabic Series, and E. J. W. Gibb Memorial Series, n.s. 19 (2 vols.; London: Luzac, 1954).

——, *Rhetoric*
Talkhīṣ al-khaṭābah [Paraphrase of Aristotle's *Rhetoric*], ed. Muḥammad Salīm Sālim (Cairo, 1967).

Avicenna, *Metaphysics*
Ibn Sīnā, *al-Shifā': al-Ilāhiyyāt*, ed. G. C. Anawati *et al.* (2 vols.; Cairo, 1960).
Healing: Metaphysics X, trans. Michael E. Marmura, in *MPP*, pp. 98-111 (P).

Farabi, *Aphorisms*
Al-Fārābī's Fuṣūl Muntazaʿah (Selected Aphorisms), ed. Fauzi M. Najjar (Beirut, 1971).
The Fuṣūl al-Madanī of al-Fārābī (Aphorisms of the Statesman), ed. and trans. D. M. Dunlop, University of Cambridge Oriental Publications, no. 5 (Cambridge: Cambridge University Press, 1961).

——, *Attainment*
Kitāb taḥṣīl al-saʿāda, in *Rasā'il* (Hyderabad, 1345/1926).
The Attainment of Happiness, Part I of *Alfarabi's Philosophy of Plato and Aristotle*, trans. Muhsin Mahdi, rev. ed. (Ithaca: Cornell University Press, Agora Paperback Editions, 1969).
The Attainment of Happiness, trans. Muhsin Mahdi, in *MPP*, pp. 52-82 (P).

——, *Enumeration*
Iḥṣā' al-ʿulūm, La statistique des sciences, ed. Osman Amine (2d ed.; Cairo, 1948).
The Enumeration of the Sciences, trans. Fauzi M. Najjar, in *MPP*, pp. 22-30 (P).

——, *Plato*

Falsafat Aflāṭun, Alfarabius De Platonis Philosophia, ed. (with Latin version) Franz Rosenthal and Richard Walzer, Corpus Platonicum Medii Aevi, Plato Arabus, ser. 2, vol. 2 (London: Warburg Institute, 1943).

The Philosophy of Plato, Part II of *Alfarabi's Philosophy of Plato and Aristotle,* trans. Muhsin Mahdi, rev. ed. (Ithaca: Cornell University Press, Agora Paperback Editions, 1969).

——, *Plato's Laws*

Talkhīṣ nawāmīs Aflāṭūn, Alfarabius Compendium Legum Platonis, ed. (with Latin version) Francesco Gabrieli, Corpus Platonicum Medii Aevi, Plato Arabus, ser. 2, vol. 3 (London: Warburg Institute, 1952).

——, *Political Regime*

Kitāb al-siyāsā al-madaniyya, Al-Fārābī's The Political Regime, ed. Fauzi M. Najjar (Beirut: Imprimerie Catholique, 1964).

The Political Regime, trans. Fauzi M. Najjar, in *MPP,* pp. 31-57 (P).

——, *Virtuous City*

Risāla fī ārāʾ ahl al-madīna al-fāḍila, Alfarabi's Abhandlung der Muster-staat, ed. Friedrich Dieterici (Leiden: Brill, 1895; reprinted 1964).

Der Musterstaat von Alfārābī, German trans. by Friedrich Dieterici (Leiden: Brill, 1900).

Ibn Ṭufayl, *Ḥayy*

Ibn Ṭufayl, *Ḥayy Ibn Yaqzan, Hayy ben Yaqdhân, Roman Philosophique d'Ibn Thofaïl,* ed. and French trans. by Léon Gauthier (2d ed.; Beirut: Imprimerie Catholique, 1936).

Hayy the Son of Yaqzan, trans. George N. Atiyeh, in *MPP,* pp. 134-162 (P).

Maimonides, *Astrology*

"The Correspondence between the Rabbis of Southern France and Maimonides about Astrology," ed. Alexander Marx, *Hebrew Union College Annual,* 3 (1926): 311-358. The text of Maimonides' letter appears on pp. 349-358.

Letter on Astrology, trans. Ralph Lerner, in *MPP,* pp. 227-236.

————, *Guide*

Dalālat al-ḥāʾirīn (Sefer Moreh nebhukhim), ed. S. Munk, rev. Issachar Joel (Jerusalem: Junovitch, 5691/1931). The page numbers of the *editio princeps* of S. Munk, *Le Guide des Égarés* (Paris, 1856-1866), appear in the margins of this edition.

The Guide of the Perplexed, trans. Shlomo Pines (Chicago: University of Chicago Press, 1963).

————, *Yemen*

Moses Maimonides' Epistle to Yemen, ed. Abraham S. Halkin, English trans. by Boaz Cohen, Louis M. and Minnie Epstein Series, vol. 1 (New York: American Academy for Jewish Research, 1952).

Glossary

A note of caution: a glossary is not a table of simple equivalents. A term's many associations and meanings in a given language often are not carried over to another tongue.

Following each English term listed below are: (1) the manuscript's Hebrew term or terms being rendered thereby; (2) in brackets, the Arabic term or terms Averroes presumably used; and (3) where appropriate, and also in brackets, the corresponding Greek term in the *Republic*.

Active intellect *śekhel pō'ēl* [*'aql fa''āl*]
Affective *hipa'alūthī* [*infi'ālī*]
Appetite (*see also* Desire) *hith'ōrerūth* [*shahwa*] [*epithymia*]
Argument (*see also* Speech *and* Statement) *ma'amar* [*kalām; qawl*] [*logos*]
Aristocracy *ro'shiyūth ha-ṭōbhīm; tigbōreth ba'al ha-ma'alah* [*ri'āsa imāmiyya*]
Art; Craft *mal'akhah* [*ṣinā'a*] [*technē*]
Bringer of nomos; Legislator *maniaḥ nimūs* [*wāḍi' al-nāmūs*] [*nomothetēs*]
Chief *ro'sh* [*ra'īs*] [*archōn*]
Coercion *mī'ūs* [*ikrāh*]
Cogitation *maḥshabhah* [*fikr*] [*logismos*]
Compulsion *hekhraḥ* [*qasr*]
Courage *amīṣūth; gebhūrah* [*murū'a; iqdām*] [*andreia*]
Craftsman; Artisan *ūman* [*ṣāni'*] [*dēmiourgos*]
Democracy *medīnah qehaliyyith; medīnah qibūṣīth; ro'shiyūth qibūṣ hamōniyy* [*madīna jimā'iyya*]
Demonstrative *mofthī* [*burhānī*]

Desire (*see also* Appetite)   *ta'avah; teshūqah*   [*shawq*]   [*epithymia*]

Dialectical   *niṣūḥī*   [*jadalī*]

Disease (*see also* Illnesses *and* Sickness)   *ḥōlī*   [*maraḏ*]

Disposition   *tekhūnah; hakhanah*   [*hay'a; isti'dāḏ*]   [*ēthos*]

Domestic   *bē(y)tī*   [*manzilī*]   [*oikeios*]

Elect few   *yeḥīdīm sgulōth*   [*khawāṣṣ*]

End of man   *takhlīth enūshīth; takhlīth ha-adam*   [*ghāya insāniyya*]

Enlarged thought   *gedōl ha-maḥshabhah*   [*kabir al-nafs*]   [*megaloprepeia*]

Equality   *shivūy*   [*musāwāt*]   [*isotēs*]

Erotic desire   *ḥēsheq*   [*'ishq*]   [*erōs*]

Erring cities   *medīnōth ṭō'ōth*   [*mudun ḏālla*]

Fable (with connotation of riddle or parable)   *ḥīdah*   [*laghz*]   [*ainigma*]

Final cause   *takhlīth*   [*ghāya*]

Free; Free-born   *benēy ḥōrīn*   [*aḥrār*]   [*eleutheroi*]

Generally accepted opinions   *mefūrsamōth*   [*mashhūrāt*]

God   *ha-ēl*   [*allāh*]   [*theos*]

Governance   *hanhagah*   [*tadbīr*]

Guidance   *hayysharah*   [*irshāḏ*]

Habit   *qinyan*   [*malaka*]

Habitude   *minhag*   [*minhāj*]

Happiness   *haṣlaḥah*   [*sa'āda*]   [*eudaimonia*]

Hedonistic   *ta'anūgī*   [*khissa*]

Human beings; Humans   *benēy adam*   [*nās*]   [*anthrōpoi*]

Human Laws   *tōrōth enūshiyōth*   [*sharā'i' insāniyya*]

Humors   *lēyḥōth*   [*akhlāṭ*]

Ignorant cities   *medīnōth sekhalōth*   [*mudun jāhaliyya*]

Illnesses (*see also* Disease *and* Sickness)   *ḥala'īm*   [*amrāḏ*]

Imagination   *dimyōn*   [*khayāl*]   [*eikasia*]

Imitation   *ḥiqūy*   [*ḥikāya*]   [*mimēsis*]

Immortality   *hisha'arūth*   [*baqā'*]

Individual   *īsh*   [*shakhṣ*]

Inquiry   *'iyyūn*   [*naẓar*]

Intellect   *śēkhel*   [*'aql*]   [*nous*]

Intelligible   *mūśkal*   [*ma'qūl*]   [*noēton*]

Investigation   *ḥaqīrah*   [*faḥṣ; istiqṣā'a*]   [*zētēsis*]

Judge   *shōfēṭ; dayyan*   [*qāḍī; ḥākim*]   [*dikastēs*]

Jurisprudence   *mishpaṭ*   [*fiqh*]

Justice *shivūy* [*'adl*] [*dikaiosynē*]

Law *tōrah* [*sharī'a*]

Lawgiver *ba'al ha-tōrah; maniah ha-tōrah* [*shāri'; wādi' al-sharī'a*]

Legal inquiry *'iyyūn tōriyy* [*nazar shar'ī*]

Liberality *nedībhūth* [*karam; jūd*] [*eleutheria*]

Lordship *adnūth* [*ghalaba*]

Love (being well-disposed toward someone or something) *ahabhah* [*mahabba*]

Man (= male) *īsh* [*rajul; mar'*] [*anēr*]

Man *adam* [*insān*]

Men; People *anashīm* [*qawm*]

Moderation *yir'ath hēt'* (literally, sin-fearing) [*qasd*] [*sōphrosynē*]

Money (*see also* Property *and* Wealth) *mamōn; ma'ōth* [*al-dirham wa al-dīnār*] [*chrēma*]

Moral virtues *ma'alōth midothiyōth* [*fadā'il khulqiyya*]

Multitude *hamōn* [*jumhūr*] [*hoi polloi; to plēthos*]

Natural disposition *yesīrah* [*jabala*] [*ēthos*]

Necessity-cities *medīnōth hekhrēhiyōth* [*mudun darūriyya*]

Oligarchy *medīnah mamōniyyith; sarūth mamōniyy; ro'shiyūth ha-anashīm ha-me'atīm; ro'shiyūth ha-pahūth; hanhagath ba'alēy ha-pehīthūth* [*madīnat al-nadhāla*]

Opinion *da'ath* [*ra'y*] [*doxa*]

Perfection *shlēmūth* [*kamāl*]

Persuasive *sipūqī* [*iqnā'ī*]

Pleasure *'arēbhūth; ta'anūg* [*ladhdha*] [*hēdonē*]

Populace *qahal* [*'āmma*] [*dēmos*]

Practical *ma'asī* [*'amalī*]

Pretenders to philosophy *mithpalsefīm* [*tafalsuf*]

Primacy *ro'shiyūth* [*ri'āsa*] [*archē*]

Property *memōnōth* [*tharwa*] [*ousia*]

Prophet *nabhī'* [*nabī*]

Reason *sēkhel; midbar; dibūr* [*'aql*] [*nous; logos*]

Reasoning *heqēsh* [*qiyās*]

Rhetorical *halasī* [*balāghī; khatābī*]

Rulership *sarūth; ri'shōnūth* [*ri'āsa*] [*archē*]

Science *hakhmah* [*'ilm*] [*epistēmē*]

Scientific *mada'ī* [*'ilmī*]

Glossary

Self-control   *amitath ha-da‘ath* (literally, true opinion)   [*ḍabṭ al-nafs*] [*enkrateia*]

Sickness (*see also* Disease *and* Illnesses)   *maḥalah*   [*maraḍ*]

Solitary, a   *mith'aḥēd*   [*mutawaḥḥid*]

Sophistic   *haṭ'a'ī*   [*mughāliṭī; mūhim*]

Soul   *nefesh*   [*nafs*]   [*psychē*]

Speech (*see also* Argument *and* Statement)   *ma'amar*   [*kalām; qawl*] [*logos*]

Spiritedness   *ka‘as*   [*ghaḍab*]   [*thymos*]

Statement (*see also* Argument *and* Speech)   *ma'amar*   [*kalām; qawl*] [*logos*]

Statesman   *ba‘al hanhagah*   [*siyāsī; ṣāḥib al-siyāsa*]

Story   *sipūr*   [*mathal*]   [*mythos*]

Teaching   *limūd*   [*ta‘līm*]

Theoretical   *‘iyyūnī*   [*naẓarī*]

Thought   *sebharah*   [*fikra*]   [*dianoia*]

Timocracy   *medīnah ba‘alath ha-kabhōd; medīnah ha-kebhōdiyyith; ro'shiyūth ha-kabhōd; hanhagah ba‘alath ha-kabhōd; hanhagah ha-kebhōdiyyith; qibūṣ ba‘al ha-kabhōd; qibūṣ ha-kebhōdiyy*   [*madīnat al-karāma*]

Tyranny   *medīnath ha-niṣūaḥ; niṣūaḥ*   [*madīnat al-taghallub*]

Unexamined opinion   *teḥilath ha-da‘ath*   [*bādi' al-ra'y*]

Vice   *peḥīthūth*   [*radhīla*]   [*kakia*]

Virtue   *ma‘alah*   [*faḍīlah*]   [*aretē*]

Wealth (*see also* Money *and* Property)   *mamōn*   [*tharwa; yasār*]   [*ploutos*]

Wisdom   *ḥakhmah*   [*ḥikma*]   [*sophia*]

Index

N. B. The page numbers are those of the Hebrew text in Rosenthal, which appear in the left-hand margins of the present volume.